MEMORIES
OF A PORTREE KID

by

Ian George Macdonald

Grosvenor House
Publishing Limited

All rights reserved
Copyright © Ian George Macdonald, 2015

The right of Ian George Macdonald to be identified as the author of this
work has been asserted in accordance with Section 78
of the Copyright, Designs and Patents Act 1988

The book cover picture is copyright to Ian George Macdonald

This book is published by
Grosvenor House Publishing Ltd
28-30 High Street, Guildford, Surrey, GU1 3EL.
www.grosvenorhousepublishing.co.uk

This book is sold subject to the conditions that it shall not, by way of
trade or otherwise, be lent, resold, hired out or otherwise circulated
without the author's or publisher's prior consent in any form of binding or
cover other than that in which it is published and
without a similar condition including this condition being imposed
on the subsequent purchaser.

A CIP record for this book
is available from the British Library

ISBN 978-1-78148-391-6

"The terror o' the Heilan glens -
that was the Portree Kid

Hee-durum-ho ... Hee-durum-hey ...
The Teuchter, that cam, frae Skye."

In loving memory of my dear friend,
teacher, colleague and neighbour
Christine M. MacLean

Acknowledgements

Several people and organisations deserve to be acknowledged and thanked for their help in the production of this book.

Gordon Willoughby for his excellent cover picture 'From Shore to Storr'.

Murdo Beaton for help with Gaelic spelling and permission to use his tale about Colonel Jock.

The late Chrissie MacSween for the story about my grandfather.

Ella Liley for her information on 'Old Portree'.

John MacKinnon, 'Erisco', for his interesting mementoes.

Professor Norman Macdonald for his many erudite snippets and his 'Great Book of Skye' which is a mine of information.

Drew Millar and Mike MacDairmid for refreshing my memory with their 'Misty Memories' talk to the Portree Local History Society.

Colleagues on the History Society Committee for interest and encouragement.

'Jan' Nicolson for permission to photograph the retro-bicycles in his Redbrick Café.

James Nicolson, Glenvaragill for his drawing of the 'New Portree High building' published in the 1969 School Magazine.

Several pictures and 1960s shop advertisements are copied from the 1968 and 1969 School Magazines. Thanks for permission to use these, and an early print of a drawing of Portree, go to The Robert MacDonald Memorial Trust.

My sister Christine Thomson for correction of spelling, punctuation and the occasional politically incorrect remark.

My brother Sorley for helpful comments and further corrections.

Donald Macdonald at Aros for his encouragement and invitation to be part of the Isle of Skye Book Festival.

The ladies at Portree's Archive Centre who look after this wonderful asset which is of such benefit to the village. They are always keen to help even when the requests are unusual!

All the staff at Grosvenor House Publications for their cooperation with this, my fourth book entrusted to their capable hands.

Finally, many thanks to the people of Portree for putting up with me, man and boy!

In spite of all this cooperation, the finished product has not been seen by anyone else, so any errors which remain are entirely my own.

Foreword

I began this book in order that both my children and grandchildren and those of my brother Sorley would know something of their ancestry. Our family was indeed privileged to have been brought up by loving parents on the Isle of Skye in a time of relative prosperity, in a caring environment, surrounded by relatives and true friends who had a genuine interest and concern for our welfare, physical, mental and spiritual. Many children in this world lack some, or all, of the benefits we had, and currently have, and that should give us pause for reflection and a fellow-feeling for others. Life in Skye was not always idyllic, indeed previous generations of our family had a relatively hard life. At the National Census of 1841, my father's eight great-grand-parents lived in equally poor circumstances, as crofting/fishing families within a one mile radius in the over-crowded townships of the Braes of Portree. Most of my mother's ancestors lived in similar conditions in Bracadale and all of them strove to improve their lot in difficult times. Our circumstances and character have doubtless been forged from the beliefs and experiences of those who have gone before us.

This is my fourth book and, not surprisingly, the one that has brought back a flood of memories, mostly positive, some funny, but some sad. Many of the people mentioned here are no longer with us and this is a reminder to all readers that "here we have no continuing city". The longest life is short at best!

Inevitably we have regrets about things we said and things we did, also things we should have said and done to and for our loved ones while they were with us. Let's not make those same mistakes with those still here!

> "Let not the errors of my youth,
> Nor sins, remember'd be:
> In mercy, for thy goodness' sake,
> O Lord, remember me."
> Psalm 25 v 7

Contents

Chapter 1	Belonging	3
Chapter 2	Origins	11
Chapter 3	Pre-school Days	18
Chapter 4	Primary School	23
Chapter 5	Excursions to Braes	28
Chapter 6	Fishing	41
Chapter 7	Food and Clothing	48
Chapter 8	Names, Nicknames, Patronymics and Acronyms	60
Chapter 9	Secondary School	67
Chapter 10	Crofting History in the Parish of Portree	78
Chapter 11	Games and Sports	83
Chapter 12	Those Mean Streets	94
Chapter 13	Church Life	99
Chapter 14	Adventures and Events	104
Chapter 15	Out and About in Portree	117
Chapter 16	Those and Such as Those	131
	Afterword	139

PORTREE KID

CHAPTER 1

Belonging

"*Cò as a tha thu*" ("Where do you come from?"), asked the railway guard, as the Mallaig train laboured through Rannoch Moor, on its way to Queen Street station, taking me, as a young student, to Glasgow University in 1969. "From Portree", I replied in English, too embarrassed that my spoken Gaelic would not be up to this conversational task. "*Agus cò leis thu?*" he added, determined to link me to one of his old Skye acquaintances. "My father is George Macdonald the Electrician, you might know him." It turned out that he did not know my father but knew another George, George MacLean, our neighbour in Martin Crescent, who was caretaker at the Elgin and Margaret Carnegie school hostels and was thus aptly nicknamed 'George the Hostel'. George, of course, was a particularly well known character who puttered about Portree, on a World War II motorbike, sans helmet. His devotion to his duties (in spite of a few brushes with Scotland's salmon fishing laws) and his services as a voluntary fireman, gained him a British Empire Medal from the Queen in 1966.

I was often afterwards to reflect on that pivotal conversation, questioning myself on my reticent, monoglotal replies, but more particularly on the sense of place and belonging that we Highlanders retain in strong measure.

Yes, I come from Portree and am very proud of that fact, but, as I became established in the big city of Glasgow my answer to the first question of my belonging was, a somewhat vague, although still proud, "I come from Skye", just as the ex-pat abroad will assure his questioner of his Scottishness rather than being too parochial in naming his home town. This line of thinking reminds me of a story I heard of Braes' man, the late Rev. Ewen MacQueen, while acting as chaplain to the Forces somewhere in England during the War, he was officiously asked to show his identity card by a guardsman at the barracks' checkpoint. The officer demanded, "Where do you come from?"

"From Camustianavaig", was the reply. "And if **you** don't know where that is, it's **your** geography that's at fault!"

So what is this belonging?

I was not born in Portree.

Like most north-end Skye folk of my generation, I was born in the maternity hospital at Uig, now the SYHA Hostel. This important institution was erected in the early years of the 20th Century to provide medical attention and health care for the sick and poor in the communities of Trotternish. Later, it was taken into the NHS and was the maternity unit for north Skye, with, on average, over 100 births per year. It was built, not in Staffin, as first intended, but beside the Uig Primary School, and thereby hangs a tale.

In the early 1700s the meal mill at Stenscholl was leased to a Lochalsh man, Donald *Ruadh* Matheson, by the Clan Donald Estate. His son James, in turn, became the miller. The 1841 census shows that James had nine sons. One of these, Roderick, joined forces with his brother-in-law John Martin, of the Martins of Bealach, and they became wealthy coffee planters in the Americas. Roderick decided to grant a sum of money to the Staffin community in order to finance a hospital, but he died before the project could begin. John Martin however, then living at Treaslane, agreed to donate similar funding on condition that the hospital was built on **his** side of the Trotternish peninsula. Poor Roderick, whose idea it was, did

John Martin Memorial Hospital

not even get a mention in the name of the new building, The John Martin Memorial Hospital.

So it was here, on a cold January night in 1951 that my mother was hospitalised for the one and only time in her life, and I came into the world at Uig.

It was snowing, or so they tell me, and *An Dotair Mòr*, (Doctor Allan MacDonald, the 'big doctor', as opposed to *An Dotair Beag*, Doctor Murdo MacKinnon, the 'small doctor') suitably fortified against the cold, struggling up the steep brae to check me over, discovered that I was tongue-tied. One quick snip and my tongue has not stopped moving since!

In spite of Uig being my birthplace I feel no particular affinity with it, or loyalty to it, although I recognise it as a lovely village bay, especially so on a June evening when the summer sun sets on the Minch over North Uist and Berneray.

Home was Portree; in particular, the bungalow beside Kiltaraglen House where my brothers Duncan and Sorley were doubtless waiting to meet the potential usurper that Dad, Mum and sister Christine were bringing back in the old, black

Ford Popular car. At that time, the Kiltaraglen croft (8 acres arable and 80 acres outrun – so really a farm) was owned and intensively worked by Alec and Mary MacIntosh and their daughter Catriona who became our firm, lifelong friends. My parents' association with Kiltaraglen House, however, had begun a long time previously when the owners were Rod and Daisy MacKenzie and their family of three. Daisy, nee Porteous was my mother's aunt, sister of my grandmother Georgeina MacKinnon. Rod, the Agricultural College representative for Skye, and Daisy had previously owned Portree's Marine Hotel, which stood by the harbour (the site now occupied by the much less salubrious oil tanks).

Kiltaraglen is the old name for Portree. Historians speculate that it was named for Talorgan, an Irish monk colleague of St. Columba. My grandfather's view was that the man was 'Tara of the Glen' and that his burial site, cell or chamber (*'Cil'*) was nearby. I remember him pointing and saying, "somewhere

Kiltaraglen House

over there". Surprisingly, fifty years later, when the miss-spelt 'Kiltraglean' housing development began at the Home Farm, archaeologists were called in to investigate an ancient burial site in that same area. Coincidence - or did the old folk know more about this than we gave them credit for?

Most historians, based on information given to Johnson and Boswell on their tour of the Highlands and Islands, maintain that the little village on the north side of St.Columba's Loch was known as Kiltaraglen until the year 1540 when the name was changed to *Port an Righ*, the King's Harbour. The name change for the village came about following the visit by King James V of Scotland on his famous expedition to the Hebrides to encourage, or demand, the allegiance of the chiefs of the Highland Clans. Alexander Campbell, the Portree schoolmaster in the 1790s, when compiling the 1st Statistical Account for the parish, was of the opinion that the name was older, coming from the 13th century visit of King Haco of Norway on his return from defeat at the Battle of Largs. Recently, a former school colleague of mine, Ella Liley, has shown me some compelling evidence that the name of Portree may be even more ancient. W.J. Watson, in *'Celtic Place Names of Scotland'*, gives the alternative translation, confirmed by many Gaelic speakers: *"Portree in Skye is often pronounced in Gaelic Port-righ, as if in 'King's port', and the name is supposed to date from a visit of James V in 1540. The unsophisticated Gaelic pronunciation of Skyemen, however, is Port-righeadh, and the second part is clearly from righ or ruigh, 'fore arm', common in our place-names as 'slope' or 'ground sloping up to a hill'"*. So *Portree should be translated as the 'Port of the Slope'*. This explanation of the name certainly seems appropriate, if less romantic than the other versions!

Kiltaraglen was to be our home for a further four years, but continued to be a place that I visited most Saturdays, until well into my teenage years. I loved the company of the MacIntoshs and enjoyed learning the crofting life, as our new home was a council house in Martin Crescent where we were not permitted

This Daniell print of early Portree gives the 'slope' idea

to keep animals or grow hay and oats -- although we did dabble with potatoes, vegetables and soft fruits! It was here that big sister developed her love for plants and flowers.

Surprisingly, although I could only have been about four years old, I remember the flitting to the new house. All our goods and chattels travelled in Alistair Lockhart's aged and noisy lorry. I sat on a five-gallon oil drum and we had tomato soup for our first meal in the new home. But perhaps that is not my first memory. I have a vague recollection of feeding hens with Mary MacIntosh holding my hand, and of meeting people on the Staffin Road while being wheeled in my pushchair.

Belonging must have something to do with our earliest memories of a place, but are these truly memories or have I built them up from later thoughts, discussions and shared reminiscences? There was an old, sincerely Christian lady, Mrs Fleming, who stayed at Holly Bank, next door to Mrs Elder at Burnbrae. She gave the impression, by her state of dress and cleanliness, of being very poor, but had a tethered milking cow and kept hens. Mum would often stop for a chat. At Craig Rannoch was John MacPherson, Eddy's grandfather, next door to Miss MacMillan the Art teacher. He was always busy hoeing vegetables or tidying his garden plot, as likewise was 'Sandy

Mòr' Matheson who lived at Mill Road. In later life my brothers convinced me that these people were all relatives of ours and so perhaps this is why I have adopted them into the memory section of my brain. John MacPherson may well have been a distant relative, as he belonged to the MacPhersons of Lower Ollach, from where my paternal grandmother came. 'Sandy *Mòr'* certainly was my paternal grandfather's first cousin, but the tentative family connection with Mrs Fleming, or her late husband, was almost certainly a fiction perpetrated by my older siblings. They concocted a story in connection with Sir Alexander Fleming, discoverer of penicillin, and Sir James Young Simpson, pioneer of antiseptic surgery, and claimed family connections to both famous scientists (my mother's paternal grandmother was a Margaret Young). Of such concoctions of ingredients are memories made!

Much to Mum's pleasure our new house, number 12, was immediately next door to her school and university friend, Mary Nicolson at number 11, now Mrs Michie, the formidable teacher of Primary 6 at the local school. Her husband Johnnie was the ambulance driver and 'George the Hostel's wife' Joey was the

Portree's Ambulance in the 1950s

ambulance nurse. That's why the local ambulance (I was sure it was a beige colour) took up residence on our street.

Our other next door neighbours were Captain and Mrs Mairi MacKenzie and their two sons, Donald and Iain. Captain MacKenzie was one of the three 'ancient mariners' who rented out rowing boats to tourists and local teenagers at the harbour, smoked pipes and reminisced on their deep-sea days.

Just round the corner on Stormy Hill lived my Mum's half-sister, Auntie Isa. With these ties of consanguinity and a precious web of friends and acquaintances my family was wrapped in a cocoon of **belonging.**

Auntie Isa's house was the smaller one, second on the left. She is here standing at its door with her husband Angus MacLeod who had passed away before I was born.

CHAPTER 2

Origins

So why was our family in Portree? Both Mum and Dad were Skye people. True, Dad had been born in 1908 in the south of Scotland and spent his early years in Greenock to where both his parents had moved, in an effort to find work on Clydeside. It is said that the prevalence of Skye folk on the River Clyde gave them the title of the Skye Navy. Like so many of the families of Portree parish, those who had not emigrated overseas to east or west, made their way to the cities of the south of the country in order to make some sort of a living. Conditions in Skye continued to be very harsh in spite of the positive provisions of the Crofters Holding Act of 1886. Samuel Macdonald of Camustianavaig and Mary MacQueen of Lower Ollach, born less than a mile apart, met again in the Clydeside town and married. Their son, my father, George, named after his paternal grandfather, was the eldest of a family of eight. Immediately after World War I, at the age of ten, with too many mouths to feed in Greenock and the pressing need for a young boy's help on the croft in Skye, Dad was sent north to assist his granny at Lower Ollach. The grandparents had lost two sons, John (*Iain Beag*), drowned at sea in 1912 and Peter, a victim in the trenches of the Great War, in 1917. Grandfather, Angus MacQueen, was suffering from long-term ill health and died in 1920. There was much work needed on the croft, but education could not be neglected. Fearful of being regarded as the city boy, Dad daily hid his boots behind the dyke on his way to the Braes school, to be like

Braes School – pupils and teachers. Dad is the third boy from the left in the back row

his barefooted school friends. On leaving school at 14, he soon returned south to learn his electrician's trade with Hurry Brothers of Greenock. He was accompanied by his Skye first cousin and best friend George Robertson from Waterloo, Broadford, who also was to learn his trade on the Clyde, but as a carpenter like his Uncle Samuel.

Mum, Jessie MacKinnon, was born in 1909 at Craiglea, Struan, the eldest daughter of a family of eight, although her father, Duncan MacKinnon had a son, Peter John and two daughters from a previous marriage. His first wife, Jessie, nee Stewart died in 1900 and Duncan struggled for six years, with the help of Jessie's parents, to bring up the three children. Since beginning to write this book, a good friend, Chrissie MacSween, divulged to us a tale told her by her late father. Duncan MacKinnon while looking after his sheep on the croft at lambing time found great difficulty in getting a certain ewe to accept an orphan lamb. This was most unusual, as he had been successful in this task on many occasions. As a lay-preacher and spiritually exercised, he realised that this incident was meant to teach him. For some time he had been contemplating whether to ask a certain lady for her hand in marriage, but realised that she, like the ewe, would not be suitable to adopt his children. In 1906 he married a younger lady, Georgina nee Porteous from Vatten House. She and his two daughters took to each other like sisters. As you can imagine, times were also particularly hard for this crofting household. Peter John, a young man who would have been expected to help in providing for the family, died at Bedford Barracks in the terrible outbreak of measles which claimed the lives of many of the First World War soldiers, suddenly thrust into contact with diseases for which they had no immunity. In spite of enormous difficulties Duncan and his brother Neil, both master joiners, were able to build two semi-detached houses, Craiglea and Craigard, for their families. Recently we have discovered that the main stuctural beam which supports the upper storeys, came from the ship 'Yemassee' which foundered in Loch Bracadale on a stormy night in 1859. The binnacle from this vessel forms the collection plate in the local church where Duncan was the lay-preacher. Education, as in Braes, was also important to folk on the west of Skye and Mum studied at Struan Primary, then Portree Secondary School and succeeded in getting a bursary to go on and matriculate in Glasgow University in 1927. Due to her mother having to undergo major surgery and her father's serious illness, she was not able to complete her MA degree and had to return to family responsibilities in Skye. Following grandfather's death in 1931, she again went south, this time to the Free Presbyterian Manse of Greenock where her aunt Margaret, wife of the Rev. James MacLeod, and profoundly deaf, welcomed her assistance with her young family. Mum also took work in a Greenock Post Office as a clerk.

So it was here, in Greenock, that these two Skye exiles, my Mum and Dad met, in similar fashion to my father's parents, through their church attendance. They married in July 1937 at Kyle of Lochalsh to be convenient for Skye relatives and, anticipating the fashion to come in their grandchildren's day, went overseas for their honeymoon – to the Island of Raasay!

Home for them continued to be Greenock until World War II began to dictate their future. Christine and Duncan were born in Greenock, but then evacuation of women and children was called for, first to the safety of Tighnabruaich in Argyllshire, accompanied by granny during the Clydebank blitz, but then back to Skye for my brother Sorley's birth. Meanwhile the men, in reserved occupations, had to work on refitting essential naval ships by day and acting as firefighters by night.

My brother Sorley was born in Struan, Skye. As the War proceeded to a satisfactory conclusion, the family moved back to Greenock where my two older siblings began their education at Finnart Primary School. Post-war employment prospects not being very encouraging, and rationing a constant concern for the young family, Dad brought them back again to Skye where they lived in his grandparents' house at Lower Ollach, Braes. Christine and Duncan attended Braes School, as their father had done, until it closed in 1948. As employment prospects were no better in the north, and as an opportunity arose with his old employers, Hurry Brothers, Dad went back south for a short time, leaving the family on the croft.

It was a combination of accident and opportunity which ensured that Dad came back to Portree. First, while walking on the pavement of a Greenock street, he was knocked down by a young man who had taken his parents' car for a joyride. After some weeks of hospitalisation, George returned home to Skye to recuperate. Several of Skye's 'big houses' were converting their 'tilley' lighting systems to electricity, supplied by diesel generators. Dad's electrician qualifications and experience were suddenly in demand. He took employment with Neil Beaton, who ran the Skye Transport firm and was branching out into the new-fangled electrical business. Soon Dad ventured to become self-employed and took on the training of several apprentices, young lads keen to get qualifications in anticipation of the start of the planned Storr Lochs Power Station. The 'ordinary folk' were now to have electricity in their homes. A brief attempt at running an electrical shop in Wentworth Street showed him that this was not his forte. The practical side, wiring houses, shops and hotels was the way forward. This venture was to be his life work until it was cut short in 1971.

The first jobs of course came from those who could best afford to be connected to the mains, as the wiring of the new Council housing schemes was contracted to mainland firms. My father always had words of praise for the Hillary Family of Lynedale House, Tayinloan House and Edinbane Lodge whose contracts, contacts and kindness ensured his employment for many years. Major General Harry MacDonald at Redcliff House and Colonel Jock at Viewfield also had their properties wired or rewired by Dad. He was employed for a short time at Dunvegan Castle and even installed electric lights, though no heating, in the dungeon! He found that Dame Flora MacLeod, the then Chief (28th), although a redoubtable lady, was very charming, and had a ready sense of humour. On discovering that his surname was Macdonald, she asked, *"Are you not afraid we will lock you in?"* *"No! As long as you don't try to marry me to a MacLeod"*, was his reply. This response referred to an old tale where a Macdonald prisoner was supposedly offered the choice of marrying a rather ugly sister of an early Chief, or the death penalty. The Macdonald's reply was, *"Give me the rope!"*

Electricians as well as Plumbers are sometimes called out in emergency. One night, Dad woke up to the ringing of the telephone and, on trudging sleepily downstairs, was greeted by a concerned, eccentric, aristocratic customer. Mr Dundas of Corry Lodge, Broadford was on the line. *"Mr Macdonald, can you come down quickly, I've lost my pyjama trousers!"* After a long pause for laughter, while holding a hand over the telephone mouthpiece, Dad asked what he meant. Apparently Mr Dundas had been warming his night clothes in front of an electric fan heater and the trousers had become entangled in the fan. The advice given was to switch off the offending device at the mains, remove the plug and collect another pair of pyjamas from the drawer. The heater could be repaired and the garment retrieved at a more reasonable hour on a later date. This incident was recited with renewed amusement many times in our family.

In the second half of the 1960s when I was of an age to be a help rather than a hindrance, Dad took me with him during school holidays. I was suitably small and supple to crawl into difficult places pulling out old lead-sheathed cables or poking new plastic covered ones up through the floorboards or behind the skirting-boards. During these excursions I visited several interesting houses. Lynedale was completely rewired. This 'stately home' was once the residence of the 3rd Lord Napier of Magdala, which he had purchased from the family of an Alexander MacDonald who had made his name in the construction industry. This gentleman, like so many before and since, had to leave Skye to seek employment in the south. With diligence and application, he worked his way upwards until he was managing some of the most important civil engineering projects in Scotland. He built several bridges throughout the country and employed Skyemen whenever possible. Many spoke highly of his consideration and treatment of his employees. His firm helped to build the Highland Railway from Dingwall to the west. In particular, he took charge of the section between *Strome Ferry* and *Kyle of Lochalsh* and blasted through the solid rock at *Creag Dallaig*. This stretch was once called *'the most expensive 12 miles of railway in the world'*. It is now recognised as one of the most enchanting!

Another of these welcome visits was to the home of Mr Pullen. He had recently built his house with its foundations virtually **in** Loch Fada, one of the Storr lochs. As a keen trout fishing fan I dreamed about the delights of fishing from the bedroom window. This was my ideal home! In the living-room I was fascinated by the head and skin of the tiger that had led to the amputation of the gentleman's left leg. There was also a stand for walking-sticks and umbrellas made from the lower leg of the Indian elephant on which he had been transported on his safari excursions.

It did not occur to me to follow in my father's footsteps and serve my time as an apprentice electrician, as I knew that he only made a sufficient wage to keep his family clothed and fed. While we never lacked for the necessities and always had a week's holiday on the mainland each summer, we were by no means well-off. Dad, by all accounts, was an excellent electrician but was too soft-hearted to be a business man. Like most Skye youngsters we were encouraged to gain school qualifications and 'better ourselves'. The downside of this advice was the inevitability that we must leave Skye to seek advancement and employment. I was keen to see the 'bright lights' but was soon to realise that, having seen them, I could live without them. Skye would always be home!

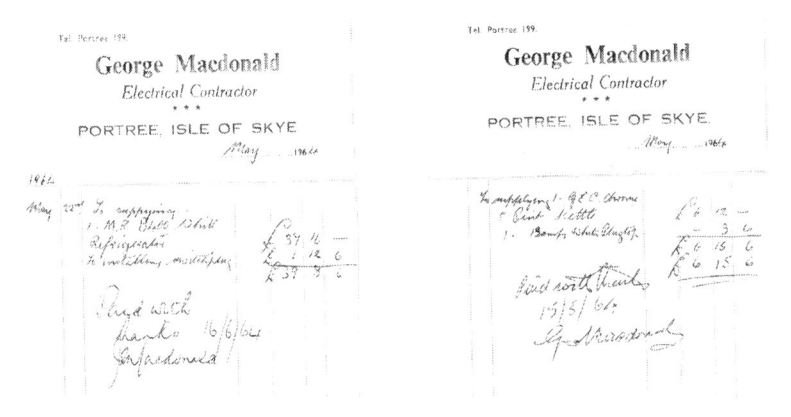

£37 – 16s for a refrigerator and £6 – 12s for an electric kettle could not have given Dad much of a profit. Thanks to John MacKinnon, 'Erisco' for the copies of the invoices.

Chapter 3
Pre- School Days

"There are no 'characters' nowadays, as there were when we were young." How often do we hear these sentiments expressed? But of course there are, we just do not appreciate them until we look back. 'Characters', of course, come in all shapes and sizes, good and bad and I confess that I will chicken-out when it comes to being explicit about some of the 'bad characters' I came across in my youth. While my readers would love to hear 'the juicy bits', fear of repercussions from offended relatives and possible libel actions mean that I will have to deny requests for real names! I may use pseudonyms, but Portree folk will doubtless know who I mean!

I'm sure that most of these 'characters' were around for much of my childhood, but I'm going to mention them in some sort of chronological order based on when I first came across them.

I was introduced to my first 'character' early on in life. He was 'Willie the Barber', William Fraser, and I became a client of his from pre-school days. I continued to have a regular haircut in his shop, on Douglas Row, until teenage embarrassment dictated that I shift my allegiance to young, trendy 'Billy the Barber', William Grainger. Old Willie had a stutter, not only in his speech but in his scissors! When one of his waiting customers engaged him in conversation, the 'victim' on the barber's chair was reduced to a quivering wreck, as the flying, snipping weapons threatened to remove an ear! I say – 'on the barber's chair' – but my early memories are of being perched on a short green-painted plank resting on the chair arms, which raised me precariously to an acceptable height for being 'operated upon'.

Willie's shop was also the only place in Portree where records could be bought. By records I mean music, long before the days of downloads, CDs, cassette tapes or even reel to reel tapes. These were vinyl or the even older hard plastic records.

In later years I was to appreciate that Willie was a keen golfer who had a regular game with the other shopkeepers on a Wednesday afternoon. Wednesday was Portree's early-closing day. These were times prior to manic commercialisation, when there was a sensible and leisurely attitude to shop life in the village. I'm reminded that Willie lived in a Council House at Park Road, next to the King George V Park. These houses are long gone and the pre-school nursery is in, what was Willie's vegetable garden. I can clearly remember him trimming his wife's washing-green with a push-mower – a busman's holiday. Even his mowing action was staccato!

In 1954, my uncle Rev. John Angus Macdonald, a Harris man, married to Barbara, my mother's sister, became the minister in Raasay, having previously been in Applecross. His translation there, led to our family making adventurous trips across to our neighbouring island. My first sea voyage across the sound was on the good ship Loch Nevis. At the Portree harbour each passenger was required to pay 'pier dues' and the person authorised to collect the fee of 2d (two old pennies) was John MacPherson, *Shonnie Beag a Chidhe* (little John of the pier), also affectionately known as 'Tuppence', for obvious reasons. He was a thoroughly pleasant man who always greeted us with a friendly smile. He lived in Fraser Crescent, a few houses along from 'Whistling Freddy the Joiner' (Freddy Jagger) another of life's cheerful people who seemed to brighten the village with his melodious tunes and upbeat conversation.

Next to Willie the Barber's shop was a large sign, 'Ian Stewart – Ladies & Gents' Tailor'. Through the large picture window it was sometimes possible to see the tailor, cross-legged on his table cutting, sewing and blethering. I say, sometimes, because there was often a group of bystanders, inside the shop, blocking your view as they caught up with the latest village gossip.

Then there was the Dairy, also on Quay Street. We would call there for extra milk if we had underestimated our order for the number of glass bottles delivered daily to our door by 'Calum the Milkman'. All Portree's milk came from the Home Farm cows. This fascinating place was always full of steam from the bottle-washing machine and water flowed out the door onto the street. Sarah would be there with her wellies, rubber gloves and apron, busily moving crates from place to place. She was another bright personality who always made one feel welcome.

I remember the pier area as a hive of activity as goods were constantly arriving, courtesy of David MacBrayne, on the daily steamer service and the weekly cargo boat, and being distributed by his vans and lorries to all the townships of north Skye. Furniture, agricultural supplies, dry goods, food stuffs and the mails all came by sea from the railheads at Kyle of Lochalsh or Mallaig, or direct from Clydeside. The characters I remember working at the pier were 'Cron' Nicolson, 'Bash' MacKinnon and the Glasgow man John Currie. Currie, a fanatical Rangers supporter, was reputed to be very strong and was often to be seen hauling large boxes or transporting sides of beef on his broad shoulders. He and his wife Nan were said to purchase a phenomenal quantity of eggs for pickling for winter consumption. On one occasion John was to become incandescent when someone painted his York Drive house-gate green and white. The blame inevitably fell on his MacBrayne's colleague Finlay MacRae.

It was probably at one of my early and frequent visits to Willie the Barber that I first took notice of the coal puffers, boats that slid quietly into Portree Bay at high tide and rested gently on the sandy bottom by the harbour as the tide went out.

Stormont's lorry filling up at Portree Harbour

A team of strong local men was recruited to help the crew unload the many tons of coal required to feed the winter fires of our houses. Coal was relatively cheap then, and when balanced against the hard work of peat cutting, lifting, drying, carting home and stacking, many households were prepared to forego the pleasant homely peat-fire for the more convenient fuel delivered to the backdoor by Stormont or Davy MacFarlane and Sons.

Another good place to have a chat, while getting 'the messages', was Lipton's shop on Bank Street. Throughout my life this shop has metamorphosed into many guises: Lipton's, Templeton's, then, Presto, then Safeway, then Somerfield and finally Co-op. But my first memory is of the cold marble floors and counters of Lipton's, Murdo Campbell cutting red cheddar with the traditional cheese wire, Maggie from Bernisdale bustling about to gather together our list items from the shelves, John Heron and Sammy Campbell's dad (*Shonnie Lipton*) loading up the mobile shop. These early memories are certainly from my pre-school days, but I'm sure they have been augmented by the addition of multiple layers superimposed upon the original. Next door, in contrast to the activity of the grocer's shop, Maggie MacQueen in Highland Home Industries presided over a haven of calm. I remember the cane baskets of all shapes and sizes, lengths of tweed and skenes of wool. Mum was an accomplished knitter and, when we got home, I was used as 'the frame' to hold the wool hank as she unravelled the wool into balls. My only other shop memory from this time is the joy of a visit to Willie Grant's. I must have been in love with his daughter, shop assistant Marie or, was it the rectangular blocks of Walls' ice-cream which fitted neatly into their special cones that had caught my fancy?

circa 1930   circa 2000

Lipton's, Templeton's, Presto, Safeway, Somerfield and now the Co-op!

CHAPTER 4

Primary School

The 'Old' Building

Although I had plenty to stimulate and occupy me as a youngster, I was ready for the transition to the local school. At that time Inverness-shire County Council policy dictated that there should be two Primary 1 intakes, one at Easter and the other after the summer holidays. So, as my fifth birthday came in January, I joined Portree Primary School in April 1956. This was the beginning of a 50 year-long association with that school site, as the Secondary was on the same campus, until I retired from the Teaching Profession in January 2006.

My introduction to formal education was to a composite class comprising the new entrants and those 'superior' pupils who had survived since the previous August. Some of them had come to understand the concept of school bullying and put it into effect in a practical manner! I was reminded of this recently when my eye lighted on a particular lady in the local Co-op. On spotting her I immediately recalled the 'bad words' she had used to me early in week one of primary school. To be honest, I remember little of the first day, other than that several of my new classmates were weepy, upset and missing their mummies; others, me included, were doubtless putting on a brave face against the unknown. In those days there were no *Sgoiltean Àraich* or *Cròileagain* to break us in! Our Primary 1 classroom was Room 4 in the "Old Building". In later years this became one of the English classrooms, the domain of the redoubtable Alan Whiteford (Buddy), and later the benign Alister Ross. Our Primary 1 teacher was the darling Mrs Sheila Urquhart whom we loved dearly.

For Primary 2 we simply moved next-door to Room 5, which for years had been Mrs Rodina MacFarlane's ('Sparrow legs') classroom, but she had recently retired, so our teacher was a young lady who lived at Sconser and whose name, (shame on me), I can not remember. Was she married to a Maths teacher in the Secondary who had a little blue sports car? Later Room 5 was to become Miss MacDairmid's room and then the school library. For Primary 3 we moved out to the wartime horsa huts and Mrs MacLean, aunt of Ian Stewart from the hardware shop (Armadale House). Primary 4 was Jetta Ross, later to become another Mrs Maclean. I looked forward with anticipation and some trepidation to Primaries 5 and 6, as I knew Mrs Nicolson from church and Mrs Michie was our next-door neighbour. There was considerable pressure to conform and behave well, as Portree was a particularly close community at that time. Woe-betide-you if your parents heard bad things about you from the teachers or Sandy *Ruadh* and John Campbell ('Cheely') the janitors, whose duties included shovelling coal and stoking several boilers! John, whose wife, a sister of 'Donald the Hall's' wife and worked in the school canteen, was recognised for his accurate analysis of the current weather, both summer and winter, "It's cheely today!" Another janitor I recall was a character we called 'Ginger' (yes, even in those days red-heads were maligned. I notice from today's press that the MP for Inverness has been called 'a ginger rodent' by a member of the Westminster Opposition!). Strangely enough, 'Ginger's' brother, Peter Whiteford, was known as 'The Grey Hen'.

My main memories of Primary school are of the daily free milk (and seconds); the cylindrical coal stove keeping out the winter chill in Mrs Michie's corrugated-iron hut; exquisite football and shinty at the "playtimes"; figs and pink custard in the canteen — (bad memory!); learning to swim in Annie Weir's canvas pool and my favourite; athletics with Farquhar MacLean, ('The Bopper'), much later to become my great friend, neighbour and colleague. I must have been in Primary 6 when the Bopper announced that he was taking us on a trip to the Skye Gathering Hall to 'see' a football match – astonishment all round! Several of the Primary classes, but **only** the boys, were marched down the village and installed on chairs in front of a small box. I'm sure this was my first experience of television. Nobody in Portree had TV in their houses but 'Alistair Bam' the electrician had one in the shop window. It worked from an aerial he had erected on 'The Lump'. For this special occasion his aerial cable was diverted to the hall and we watched Real Madrid v Eintracht Frankfurt in the 1960 European Cup Final, which was played at Hampden Park Glasgow. This has been hailed as one of the greatest finals ever and we were engrossed with the black and white moving images. Real won by 7 goals to 3 and we learned about the great Alfredo Di Stefano whose fifth consecutive European Cup Final victory this was. Has there ever been a more all-round footballer?

For Primary 7, the 'Qually' or qualifying class, we had Mrs Hodson and hand-work with Mrs Christine MacLean.

These last two encounters inadvertently provided a link with the Secondary school as both were married to teachers we would have when we moved to the 'big school'. While in P7 I can clearly remember the day we expected the world to succumb to nuclear disaster during the Cuban Missile Crisis, and breaking John MacLeod's glasses at football. The potential consequences of both incidents seemed of equal importance to me!

Primary School days were full days. We were always busy at work and busy at play. As we had a class of 36 pupils, our teachers must also have been kept very busy both in and out of school, as we never seemed to have to wait for homework to be corrected – there was always more to do for the next day! We were indeed fortunate that our teachers were diligent, our environment was pleasant and safe, and we had every opportunity and encouragement to progress our education. Not every child is so blessed. I'm sure my own experiences were the major factor in my wishing my own children to grow up in a similar caring environment.

As I write this chapter we have had the very sad news of the passing away of our dear friend Christine MacLean, mentioned above. While Christine was one of my teachers she was also to become a close colleague when I came to teach in the High School in 1980, a caring, joyful friend and near neighbour. We will miss her cheerful good advice and opinion which we knew to be always available and generously given. A bright light has gone out in the Isle of Skye!

An interesting development which had a very positive and adventurous effect on my time at primary school was the arrival of a new pupil who was to become a firm friend. Duncan Geddes lived with his parents on the Isle of Soay. His dad was the famous Tex Geddes, former soldier and adventurer and his mum was then known in the press as the "Queen of Soay". Tex had sailed with Gavin Maxwell, author of "Ring of Bright Water" and "Harpoon at a Venture", on their shark-fishing excursions and had continued the business by purchasing the island base (see his book "Hebridean Sharker"). As Soay no longer had a primary school, because Duncan was the only school-age pupil, he had to be boarded out in Portree. He got accommodation at Park House, Bayfield with 'Calum the Postman's', mum and seemed to be always available for high jinks. He and I had a hut at the Bayfield Road-end, beside the Corrigals' boat shed. We used to heat up tins of soup in a make-shift stove fuelled by easily obtainable saw dust (mixed with a little paraffin), from the shed next door. Duncan will, no doubt, feature in further reminiscences of high adventure.

Chapter 5

Excursions to Braes

While weekdays were occupied with the enjoyment of school, Saturdays were always eagerly anticipated. Two main things could happen on a Saturday, either I made my way down the cliff path from Martin Crescent and north on the Staffin Road to a tryst with the MacIntoshs and their sheep, cattle, dogs and hens at Kiltaraglen, or we went in Dad's car the 5 miles to Braes.

The little house at Lower Ollach was now the home of Dad's Uncle John, the last of the MacQueens, my Granny's family. Uncle John seemed to me to be a very old man in those days but it is sobering to think that he was, in fact, no more than 10 years older than I am now. He had spent his life of hard work as a labourer with the firms of Tawse and Kings on various road construction contracts around the Highlands and Islands. John, 'Iain Mor' was now the tenant crofter on land that had continued in his family since before the Ollach crofts were designated as such by John Blackadder, for Lord MacDonald's Braes Estate, in 1811. As far back as 1733 our ancestor, John Nicolson, was the tacksman tenant of Nether Ollach.

The Clan Donald Rent Records show this:

"*John Nicolson of Olich being sworn and interrogated in the Irish tongue, depones that he possesses the half of one pennyland of Olich and pays yearly for the same to Sir Alexander or his factor forty merks of silver duty, two pound eight shillings scots of cess*

and two pecks of horse corn and no other casualties whatever, and this is the truth as he shall answer to God.
Cannot write."

The grandson of this John Nicolson, also a John Nicolson 'Iain Og', married Flora MacQueen. Their daughter Chirsty (*Chirsty 'n Oig*), in turn married Angus MacQueen of Achnahanaid. Chirsty and Angus were the parents of my Granny, Mary MacQueen and Grand Uncle John. Unusually, the assignation of the croft and crofthouse had come down through the female line, as new husbands moved into the little, sturdily-built cottage after marriage and took over the croft tenancy. This trend continued, as unmarried Uncle John willed the tenancy to my father; thus a Nicolson croft became a MacQueen croft and then a Macdonald croft. It seems logical therefore that I assign the tenancy to my daughter Margaret, Mrs Chiappini! My how the world has shrunk!

Chirsty 'n Oig

Uncle John and Barney

Uncle John had a few sheep as his 'souming' on the Common Grazings but had been forced by the scourge of 'the rheumatics' to sell his cows. He still had a sheepdog, Barney. Barney was not one of the more common Border Collies but a Bearded Collie, a similar, but smaller version, of the Old English Sheepdog. Like his master, Barney suffered from age-related afflictions, but was reputed to have been able to bring the township's milking cows home from the hill of an evening, while John and his neighbours remained with pails and stools, in anticipation, at the byre doors!

Indeed, the byre door was a place where Uncle John loved to stand, cutting black twist tobacco for his pipe, scraping out the dottle, while looking out towards the neighbouring township of Achnahanaid to observe the antics of *Ruaraidh* Kelly and his white horse. I often copied him by leaning on the opposite door-post as he told tales of the past. Perhaps it was from him I learned of his mother's great strength. She could carry a bole of meal (130lbs) to the house from the supplies-boat at the bottom of the croft, a distance of about 200yards, uphill! Chirsty is reputed to have been among the amazons who had fought at the Battle of the Braes – her brother James certainly was one of the five men for whose arrest a fifty strong posse of Glasgow Policemen had been recruited by the notorious Sheriff Ivory. I hope to tell more of this tale in a more convenient part of the book.

Chirsty had also, inadvertently, while carrying a load of dried bracken for cow-bedding, brought back an adder from the hill. Like the Apostle Paul, in Biblical times, she shook it off and survived! Perhaps it was this tale that gave me the fear of snakes which remains with me!

Beside Uncle John's byre was another unusual building, the boat house (*tigh 'a bhata*)! Not a house for storing a boat, but a building whose roof was an upturned, redundant and highly tarred boat. These sheds had apparently been very common in Braes but, as far as I know, Uncle John's was the last one to survive. Latterly this was his coal store as well as a repository for all sorts of instruments and tools that were interesting for small boys. There were branding-irons, gin traps, adzes, assorted chisels, donkey shoes, fence tighteners, panniers, hazel baskets, pails and saws – a fascinating place!

One of my tasks on visiting in Braes was to get the daily pail of water from the well, as, until the late 1950s there was no piped water. Indeed, even then, Uncle John could only afford, or indeed see the need for, a standpipe at the gable end of the house. I say, daily pail of water, but, if our visit was indeed on a Saturday, two pails of water were required for the weekend supply. No one in the community would even think of visiting

Tigh 'a bhata (boat house)

the well on Sabbath, The Lord's Day. Although piped water was late in arriving, all the Braes houses had electricity from the mid fifties. I remember the brown bakelite 15amp sockets and switches, although the Tilley lamps still had a place of honour for emergencies. A tale is told of the Braes lady who only switched on the electric light in the late evening so that, in the gloaming, she could find the matches to light the Tilley!

The old cast iron zebo-blackened cooking stove was the main feature in the kitchen/living-room. There was a pale green 'dresser' for the crockery and cutlery, a wooden table covered in an oilcloth and Uncle John reclined on the hard wooden bench. No wonder he spent much of his time standing at the byre door! The bench must have increased the rheumatic agony.

It comes to my memory that Uncle John decided to modernise by replacing the stove with a modern fireplace. The article was duly ordered by letter, shipped to Portree on MacBraynes' cargo boat, 'Loch Dunvegan', and delivered to Braes by lorry, along with the winter's coal supply. *Donal Beag*, next door, was entrusted with the extraction of the old and installation of the new and the whole operation seemed to take much of the summer. The open fire brightened up the previously rather gloomy room but also provided Uncle John

Donkey with peat creels

with the added feature of spittoon. His aim was amazingly accurate, as witnessed by the frequent hiss from the burning coals! Coal was indeed the main fuel used in Ollach because the near peatbanks were exhausted and others were so far up the hill that the fuel had become too difficult to transport. Until the late fifties every crofter had a donkey. These animals could carry panniers laden with peat, or were trained to pull a small cart. The last of Braes' Gaelic *Bard Baile* (village poets), *Calum Ruadh*, relates the humorous tale of how the very useful donkeys first came to Braes. I have translated a short portion of it.

> "Two spinster ladies from Gedintailor wrote a letter to a Clydeside firm ordering Kerr's Pink seed potatoes for the spring planting. Unfortunately, due to the unfamiliar English, they misspelled 'Kerr's' and omitted 'Pink'. A 'chair' duly arrived for collection at Portree pier. In high dudgeon the ladies responded with a telegram to MacFarlane Shearer, the Greenock merchant; "Please send ass required"! The dutiful supplier sent a donkey as ordered!"

Thereafter, the ubiquitous donkeys provided endless amusement in the local townships. Young lads would swap the animals in the various byres by night causing chaos and consternation among the owners and ammunition for *Tearlach a' Phost* and *Niall Ceanneach* two of the other Braes poets and satirists.

All the Ollach donkeys had gone before my time but there were still one or two in the other Braes townships. We had to content ourselves with playing with the redundant cartwheels, fixed on their strong steel axles. A pair of pram wheels served to make a four-wheeled, two-seater chariot. My friend and I bravely clambered aboard and sped down the croft in free-wheel. Following several attempts without incident, we hankered for further excitement and boldly decided to use the contraption with the large cartwheels at the front rather than at the back. As a result, of course, the 'bogey' now had no steering and had doubled its capacity for speed. Disaster for the vehicle, but our two young bodies survived the parachuting into the watery, smelly bog. Corporal punishment no doubt followed, as a discouragement from further reckless behaviour!

On every visit to Braes, it was expected that we would ceilidh on the nearest neighbours *Donal Beag* and *Annag* to the north, or *Katag* and *Coinneach* and their son Farquhar to the south. Donald MacIntosh (*Domhal Challum*) and (*Bean Dhomhail Challum*, his wife, sadly not dignified by us with a name of her own, but a lovely lady none the less!) lived to the west. In later years, *Annag's* sister Catriona and her husband Norman (*Tormaid 'n Dubh*) retired to the house immediately to the east of Uncle John's, and so the ceilidh time could be extended to a full 360 degree circuit. To refuse a cup of tea and a scone in any of the homes was regarded as an offence and so stomachs also became well-rounded! Although the houses would be regarded as primitive by today's materialistic standards, the welcome by those house-proud ladies, and their less tidy spouses, was warm and genuine.

Annag's husband was *Donal Beag* Nicolson, but the third occupant of their house was *Donal Mor*. *Donal Mor* had learning difficulties and could only use his own restricted language. His constant presence must have caused some confusion in my young mind as I was known to ask why *Annag* had two husbands. *Donal Mor* Matheson (*Donal Mor Thearlaich*) was in fact her brother. A lasting impression I have of him is his always removing his cap and reverently placing it on his knee before 'grace' was asked, prior to a meal or even a 'strupag'. These people gave glory and thanks to God even in the little things.

Donal Beag was a tailor and had a workshop by the roadside, beside their house. It was a place for passers-by to stop and blether as he peddled his Singer sewing machine or plied his hot smoothing irons. Sadly, *Donal Beag* was later to become bedridden, nursed by Annag for many years, as the result of a 'stroke'.

Donal Beag and Annag by the Tailor's Shed

Uncle John's Ollach neighbours

I was often given a few pennies to spend at Lipton's grocery van which always came to Braes on a Saturday, but if we happened to be there on a Friday, Alec Borve's van had better sweets and sold wagon-wheels and creamola foam! Friday visits could only be made in the school holidays when Mum and I would travel from Portree on the once-a week bus! The occasional Friday trip was a housekeeping task for Mum, as Uncle John's house **often** required a 'spring clean', whatever the season!

It is interesting to note, fifty years later, that Braes still gets its Friday Bus. I did feel sorry for the couple, waiting in the bus shelter on a Monday afternoon last July. They seemed upset when I told them of their four day wait for the next bus! They had brightened up considerably, however, when my car dropped them off in Portree's Somerled Square.

Occasionally the Braes' trip would have the added excitement of 'a fank'. The Lower Ollach township residents always turned out in force to ensure that all their sheep received the required treatment. Picnic baskets were organised and there was an air of festivity. The men and dogs had gone off at crack of dawn to the 'hill' to 'gather' and, with much barking, from both men and dogs, the sheep were finally penned in the fank. Flasks of tea, oatcakes and crowdie, scones and pancakes with gooseberry and blackcurrant jam, and perhaps a wee dram, were the order of the day, before operations commenced. If it was shearing time, it was the men who usually clipped with hand shears while the women rolled the fleeces and put them in bags. One woman, returning from the emancipaticed south, usurping tradition, had the audacity to put her hand to the shears and proved her worth to the surprise and acclamation of the men-folk.

The shearing was done on earth-banks constructed many years in the past for this particular purpose. The shearer sat astride the bank, or bench, and the sheep was laid on her back; three legs were tied and so the operation was leisurely, so unlike the frenetic machine-shearing practiced nowadays. Our task, as kids, was to climb into the bags to trample down the wool to make room for more. Happy days!

Dipping was another special occasion. All the sheep and lambs had to undergo the ordeal of being plunged into a bath of assorted, foul-smelling chemicals to kill off mites, ticks, lice and other unmentionables, and to keep their skins free from these for a prolonged period. The seriousness of this operation was underlined by the need to inform the local Police Station of the time and place of the township dipping so that a constable could make himself available as an observer, (if criminal investigative duties did not intervene – of course). He was supposed to jot down in his notebook, in consultation with the township clerk, the numbers of each owner's animals treated, presumably to put the fear of death into shepherds who had not made a 'clean gather' (i.e. left some sheep on the hill). He had also to ensure that the crofters completely immersed each sheep, and kept it in the tank for at least two minutes. There was a profound fear of the dreaded 'sheep scab'! Good ammunition for teasing-adults to frighten little boys who then needed to be consoled by their mothers at bedtime; "No children! You cannot catch sheep scab, orf, blackleg, braxy or any of these animal diseases. Now go off to sleep!"

No doubt the constable, although still technically 'on duty', would not feel excluded from joining in the post-dipping food and drink!

As 1960 approached, it became obvious that Uncle John could not continue to live alone and so he was taken to Portree to stay at our house until his Doctor admitted him to Gesto Hospital at Edinbane. This institution was another 'gift' to the people of Skye and 'adopted' by the NHS. The story goes as follows:

Kenneth MacLeod, son of the tacksman of Gesto, retired from an active life as a tea and indigo planter, having amassed a fortune in India, he was disappointed to be refused the purchase or rental of the former family lands from his clan chief. Instead he bought the estates of *Greshornish, Orbost, Skeabost, Skirinish and Tote,* but continued to be known as *Coinneach Mòr Gheusto* (Big Kenneth of Gesto).

As is usually quoted for Skyemen who have made good, Kenneth left for India *"with a golden guinea in his pocket and his fare paid"*, courtesy of Mrs MacDonald of Waternish. (He was luckier than Duncan MacLeod of Skeabost who set off *"with only a half-crown"*). After a year's work, Kenneth took the river boat down to Calcutta. On the way he went ashore and visited a place where an auction of the contents of a sugar factory was in progress. With his precious guinea, he bought a copper boiler, which he sold in Calcutta for £30. He then returned to the derelict sugar factory and bought it with the profit on the previous deal. This set him on the ladder to riches. Personal contacts were an added bonus — he became a close friend of the Rajah of Hutival. His return to his homeland however, was tinged with sadness when his fiancé died in Paris.

Kenneth is *'The Landlord'* in Alexander Smith's book *'A Summer in Skye'*. In fact he was Smith's wife's uncle.

Coinneach Mòr's lasting legacy was his endowment of the local hospital in 1869, the first in Skye and named *Gesto Hospital* after his birthplace. He guaranteed £800 per annum, his near neighbours Lachlan MacDonald of Skeabost £800 and MacDonald of Waternish £400, for the upkeep of the facility. For many years, not only was it important to Skye but also the Uists, as it provided the nearest operating theatre for those islands, being a two hour voyage and one hour pony-and-trap ride away! In 1948, the 12-bed hospital became part of the National Health Service and continued as a surgical unit until the late 1950s. During this time, care of some elderly folk became part of *Gesto's* duties.

Uncle John was well looked after at Gesto and I fondly remember visiting him with my dad. He continued to be allowed to smoke his beloved pipe – even in bed. Changed days now for the NHS!

At age 80, on the 23rd April 1961, Uncle John passed away and I was astonished to learn that he had remembered me, a ten year-old boy, in his Will. The explanation I was given was, "Well you are called after him you know and Ian is the Gaelic for John." I didn't know — but if I had known, I could not have enjoyed his company any better than I had!

A good friend of my parents and a highly respected Christian lady, Maggie Gillies from Staffin, who had become homeless when her employment at the Braes Post Office had ceased, came to rent Uncle John's former abode. She made it a happy home for herself for many years and we continued to be made welcome. She made wonderful griddle scones!

I was not in Braes on Saturday 16th September 1961 when Skye suffered one of its worst tragedies. Uncle John had passed away and Braes visits had become temporarily less frequent. That day I had gone north, from home to Kiltaraglen. My hero Alec MacIntosh had suffered a mild heart attack and had been told to take bed-rest for a week or two. Full of the self-importance and naivety of youth, I told my parents that I knew all the things that needed to be done on the farm, and set off to put my pride into practice. The female MacIntoshs knew better, and because the weather forecast predicted a storm, I was told that I would be most useful in chatting to Alec in his bedroom, so that he would not have occasion to look out the window, as his daughter Catriona fought bravely to tie down the hay coils with nets, ropes and stones. My task was indeed an important one, as Alec would otherwise have been up and outside to the detriment of his health and life! The hay was made safe without loss or damage but, when my father came to collect me, we learned of the terrible happening at Ollach. *Chirsty 'n Duibh*, at number 5 had been killed by the collapse of her new house.

Margaret, Katie and Chirsty Nicolson, adult daughters of the late John Nicolson, known as *Iain Dubh*, had decided to invest in one of the new Dorran houses which were then being touted around the Highlands. This was a new concept. Instead of stone or brick, the new houses were composed of pre-fabricated concrete panels, fitted together with steel bolts. The mainland workers had knocked off for the weekend, leaving windows open in the half-finished building. Fearing that the storm would cause the roof to be blown off, the sisters opened the front door to secure the premises. Disaster! The panels collapsed, killing Chirsty and injuring Katie. Margaret was fortunately unharmed and able to call for assistance. What sadness in this close-knit township! Can a community ever regain its composure after such a shock? It is truly amazing how time heals, although the scars, physical but especially mental, will always remain!

Chapter 6

Fishing

From a young age my brothers and sister began to interest me in all sorts of fishing excursions. Perhaps my first outing was to the little wooden bridge at Clachamish which led to Auntie Katie's house. Katie was the other of Mum's half-sisters. My own sister often went to visit there and I recall staying for a night or two in her company. This fishing trip was somewhat primitive but productive, if the catching of two or three inch tiddlers can be thought of as productive! We fished with line, worm and 'gold' safety pins! The little trout must have had suicidal tendencies, as we seemed to get lots. Yes, they were tiny, and no, we did not throw them back. Coated in flour and fried with Auntie Katie's culinary skills, learned as cook at 'Redcliff' and 'Viewfield', they tasted delicious. I was hooked!!

Further trout trips followed; with Sorley to the little burns in Braes, with Dad or Duncan to Braes' Loch Fada, courtesy of Major General Harry MacDonald, landlord of the Braes Estate, to the Red Burn at Greshornish, courtesy of Donald Matheson landlord of that estate, or to the Rivers Leasgeary and Cracaig, either side of Portree; all of them great fun and memorable outings. Scorry Falls on the Cracaig was a special place which conjured up the magic of the jungle and fed the imagination. The little cave behind the falls was where I would hide out if I became a wanted man! The fact that sea trout would come into the pool below the falls at high tide, no doubt helped my imagination with the problem of food security if the worst came to the worst!

Of these fishing excursions, undoubtedly the best, was one with brother Sorley to North Uist where we enjoyed wonderful trout fishing for a week.

I was a bit older when sea fishing was first mooted. Off the rocks at the mouth of the Bay, beyond the Black Rock, was a good and productive starting point. Cuddy Point in the Bay was banned while I was little, as Mum regarded it as too dangerous and she was right! Several young lads fell in over the years. Later, as a teenager, the rule was relaxed and we caught lots of little cuddies from there. Portree Pier was also a good place for these little fish but we did not eat them. An adventure at low tide, along the slippery, barnacle-encrusted beams beneath the pier convinced us that any fish caught in this area were likely to cause severe gastric problems. A fractured sewage pipe and leaking effluent from the oil-storage tanks did not encourage our pursuit of piscine haute-cuisine. If my mother had known that I was crawling, slipping and sliding under the pier, I'm sure the ban would have been re-instated and widened to exclude access to any water, salt or fresh!

One day, at school, my friend John Angus Matheson announced that his dad had bought a boat and would I like to go out with them. *Tha be ruith ach leum!*

This was a 12 foot larch on oak, clinker built, wooden boat which had seen many coats of paint. Currently it was a bright shade of green which seemed to be the 'in' colour, as several other well-known 'salts' were busily doing up their craft in like manner. Perhaps someone had acquired a job-lot of 'racing green'. We manhandled the craft down to the water from the slipway on this occasion, but the plan was to moor it on an 'endless rope'. A small fee was payable to the Moorings Committee for this privilege and the picturesque bobbing of moored craft in the bay still presents a lovely view during a Portree summer. We had many such trips over the years when mackerel seemed to be very plentiful. The eight feathered hooks were often fully loaded when pulled to the surface. Not so nowadays, when both mackerel and herring have become scarce due to human greed. We were taught not to be greedy and Tommy Matheson, much to our dismay, would often say, "That's enough for tonight boys!" On getting back to shore, the spoils were divided and shared out with neighbours and local pensioners who were most grateful. As Tommy was a local postman, he was well aware of who might be needy.

My Mum and Dad were not fans of mackerel but loved herring. These fish, the silver darlings, were netted in the late evening or early morning. Often, a pair of rowing boats was used to efficiently enclose a shoal. The best local herring fishers were the 'Dottie' brothers Angus and Donald MacLeod. They often caught sufficient to sell at the 'Corner' at the top of Quay Brae. Four wooden fish boxes-full constituted a cran. The Dotties often had more than a cran for sale at peak times of the season. Fresh herring were fried in oatmeal for dinner or 'tea'. Many local folk, in those days, had the skills to pack the herring in barrels with coarse salt to store for winter consumption. Salt herring with good 'Kerr's Pink' or 'Golden Wonder' potatoes were our usual main meal on a winter Saturday. Occasionally, however, we might have salt ling in white sauce. While the herring pickle was liquid in the barrels, the salted ling blocks were dried to a rock hard consistency. The night before use the blocks were softened and de-salted by soaking in fresh water. These fish meals were truly delicious and even writing about them now causes a watering of the mouth. As a little boy I was not so fond of **finding** bones in my fishy meals but was encouraged to persist. Nowadays I need my reading glasses when eating salt herring in order to **find** the bones!

As a teenager my boating experiences widened as further permissions were granted. Farquhar Macdonald, Uncle John's neighbour at Ollach had a fifteen foot 'MacKenzie' boat. The MacKenzie boat-building family were legendary and their boats synonymous with quality and even to mention in school that I had been out in a 'MacKenzie' boat drew attention. This may seem strange as the MacKenzie boys and girls were in the

High School and Primary School with us, as the centre of operations was at Heatherfield in Portree Bay.

As the Ollach/Achnahanaid beach was relatively rocky, manpower was required to launch Farquhar's boat. On my first trip we had Norman Bruce from Ollach and Fred Deacon from London as well as the master/owner and I. Liberally soaked, round lengths of barkless wood allowed the keel to slide gently towards the water from the boat's normal 'berth' in one of the special noosts at the top of the beach. His was the only occupied noost, although there was evidence of 6 or 7 others which would have been of use by all the township' families at the beginning of the 20th century. This was further evidence of Braes' loss of population over the years. It used to be said that a township was no longer viable when there were insufficient men to launch a boat.

Absence of manpower was Lachie Nicolson's problem when he asked my father if I could come out fishing with him on occasion. Lachie *'Ghoppie'* lived at the end of the Braes road at Peinchorran. He was a very friendly man and able gardener with a penchant for rhubarb growing. He enjoyed stopping tourist cars as they manoeuvred at the turning point and coaxed their drivers into conversation. I still can picture him, on his knees on the road, with his elbows resting on a car's open window, giving a history or geography lesson or learning about the everyday lives of his captive audience. He had a good boat and knew every rock and shoal in Loch Sligachan and the Narrows of Raasay, but there were few young men in the township who could help him launch her. It was a two-man operation and I was overjoyed to be asked .... that is, until I had come across the 'ceremony'. Lachie would never put to sea unless conditions were perfect and he had, over the years, learned to observe the swell on the *Sgeir Dhubh*. I would arrive, itching to get to the boat, but Lachie would have other ideas. "The wind is still a bit fresh but in half-an-hour it will back to the south and ease off. We'll go in and have a cup of tea."

The tea was black and strong and no sugar or milk was offered but there were crackers and crowdie. Unfortunately the white crowdie was liberally sprinkled with black specks which may, if I was feeling very positive, have been flakes of soot from his open fire, or ....! On other occasions, if the weather change was anticipated to take longer, he would announce scrambled eggs on toast or perhaps a plate of custard with his stewed rhubarb. Perhaps I had spent a sheltered childhood, but the sight of the food and its attendant contaminants, offered with true kindness, was enough to make me cringe! How different everything became when we were out in the fresh air with the little seagull engine puttering at the stern. Lachie's skill in anchoring a boat in the exact position to get pollock or saithe was uncanny. "We'll now try for the *bodach ruadh* (cod)", he would say, and we would up anchor and motor along until he had lined up the boat's bow with the chimney of *Shonnie Beag's* house, the stern with Suishnish Hill, on Raasay, and he could just see Holoman Island beyond the Aird. "This will be about right", he would say, and the heavily weighted rope would be lowered to the sea-bed. Sure enough we would catch large and small cod on the baited hooks. The after-fishing ritual was also important to Lachie. The fish were divided into three large heaps. "This is mine, the middle one is the boat's share and that's yours", he would say. "Out of my lot this *gatt* is for my brother at the Camustianavaig Post Office, and this one for Donald Nicolson at Hollybank on the Staffin Road and a couple for my own tea. From the boat's share you can drop these off for Dougal, Donald's brother and the last lot for *Peigi and Calum Ruadh*. You've got family of your own to share yours."

For years, after I had learned to drive myself, and was no longer dependant on a lift to Peinchorran, and a patient driver, willing to accommodate all my distribution appointments, I would continue to go out fishing with Lachie. When university holiday time was approaching he would phone up to my mother, feeding coins into the red Peinchorran telephone box to ask, "When is the boy coming home? Tell him to come up here and we'll go out in the boat."

Yes; these fishing diets were a joy but I didn't ever get used to the hors d'oevres!

In my early teens a neighbour, who shall remain nameless, introduced us to an unusual fishing instrument. It was made from a child's wooden yacht cut in half longitudinally. The half to be used was balanced with an outrigger system. Along the length of the half-yacht was a wire runner on which a metal ring could slide freely. In turn, the ring was connected by fishing gut from which hung at intervals, a number of trout flies and the line was controlled by the fisherman. When launched on a freshwater loch, the operator had merely to continue walking along the lochside and the 'otter', as it was called, sailed diagonally towards the centre of the loch. If a fish was caught on a fly, all that the controller needed to do was stop walking while pulling in the line. The 'otter' would then return to shore in a graceful arc so that the trout could be retrieved. On the rare occasions when no fish were biting, and sailing back along the loch's length was required, it was not even necessary to re-launch the craft, merely to allow the ring to slip along the wire and to begin walking back to the starting point. Having expressed doubts about the legality of such a system, we were assured that, as long as the number of fishing flies did not exceed seven, no law was infringed. With this doubtful assurance we proceeded to catch many tasty, pink fleshed trout on a couple of lochs, which will also remain nameless.

My final comment on fishing experiences may also lead me into possible conflict with the Law of Scotland and so are perhaps best glossed over. Poaching for salmon can be a very thrilling experience, at least so I am told! The summer after I left school, my friend John Angus and I got employment with a County Council road-tarring squad. We enjoyed the work immensely and especially the company of some of the most knowledgeable and entertaining people I have ever met. One of the many skills to be found within this group of stalwarts was one in which a tasty fish could be tickled from beneath the bank of a river and deposited under the driver's seat in the lorry, well within the allotted fifteen minute tea-break!

CHAPTER 7

Food and Clothing

They tell me that wartime rationing was still in force when I came into the world, but I remember nothing of this. My first recollection of purchased food was from the heavy tea-chests which came on the cargo boat, Loch Dunvegan, and were delivered by lorry to the cottage at Kiltaraglen. Our potatoes and vegetables came from our own very productive garden and we had a daily milk supply from the MacIntoshs' cows, and eggs aplenty from their hens. The tea-chests came from the supplying merchants on Clydeside, MacFarlane – Shearer. To be honest, I have little recollection of the food items they contained; probably the necessities of tea, sugar and flour but the emptied tea-chests made excellent playthings. One minute the tea-chest was a car, next it was a pirate ship or a tent. There was no end of fun with these containers but they did have hidden hazards as there were little nails which connected their sides to the box frame. Scratches and tears (both pronunciations!) were associated with these. Later I was to hear the letters C.O.D. in connection with parcels containing new clothes, although hand-me-down, make and mend, sewing and knitting were my mother's preferred methods of kitting us out. Cash On Delivery was the method by which the clients of *Shonnie Dhomhall Uilleam* got their new garments by post. When a C.O.D. parcel arrived the postman was authorised to accept payment for the item as well as the postage due on it. By giving the well known catalogue firm of J D Williams a patronymic, somehow **he** became personalised, a family friend just like our own local shop-keepers. I recall hearing of one *caileach* who always remembered to send a Christmas card to Mr Oxendale! Patrick Thomson, North Bridge, Edinburgh was another of Mum's favourite on-post suppliers. This firm would send two or three similar items on approval with free return for those items not required. A bonus for those of us living 'in the sticks'!

We must eat far more nowadays! How is it that we could 'do the messages' with a little basket in the fifties and sixties, albeit we went to the shops several days in a week and now do a 'big shop' perhaps once in that period? We had our milk delivered at Martin Crescent of course, so that was less to carry home in the bag, but even the volume of milk we consume nowadays seems so much more. No doubt we have been beguiled by the supermarkets, glossy advertising and our own greed. When we lived at Martin Crescent we got all our groceries at MacKinnons' Stores, which we called, Lexy's. When she retired Harry MacArthur came to take over the wee shop on Stormyhill Brae. I often went with a 'list' for Mum or for Auntie Isa. Lexy and her sister Morag were lovely people and they and their customers provided great channels of communication as well as an excellent social service. I can well remember with delight as Morag carved the middle-cut bacon with the huge manual slicing machine and the care with which she packed my purchases into the shopping bag. Prices were written onto the list in pencil, the arithmetic was swift and accurate, and payment and change were exchanged in mum's or auntie's purse so that little boys had only to carry the 'messages' home. Although Lexy's till gave a futuristic 'ping' it was by no means a calculator, simply a cash drawer. My 'payment' for this painless chore was usually a penny sweetie, of which there was a vast and bewildering selection on display in the large glass jars behind the counter. Do you remember the cinnamon-coated Tobermory Tatties, MacCowan's Toffee with the picture of a Highland cow on the wrapper, and the horribly coloured Caramac chocolate? Lexy and Morag lived with their brother on Coolin Drive and their house was the favourite destination for boys and girls at Halloween, as a selection of the shop treats was brought home for distribution.

The Co-op was on Quay Brae, in the Gladstone Buildings, and we occasionally got some of our groceries there. A favourite treat was a half dozen of their bakers' rolls. These could be bought in the shop, or collected directly from the bakery on Beaumont Crescent in the early morning. Christopher MacRae, Ian Jagger and the other bakers were happy to allow a fascinated young lad to watch the activity, as the giant mixer churned the dough and the long wooden paddle was pushed deep into the hot oven to extract the delicious smelling loaves and trays of rolls.

Another interesting feature of the Co-op was the requirement to quote the divi-number on request. Ours was 1013 and,

External and internal views of the Co-op in the Gladstone Buildings Quay Brae

although I had no idea of its purpose, I knew it was somehow important and must not be forgotten. The number must have been drilled into the deepest recesses of my brain as I still remember it when other, more important things, have long gone!

MacKinnon's Bakery was in Somerled Square, not where MacKenzie's bakery is now, but next to the Masonic Hall. 'Lala' MacKenzie worked for the MacKinnons, eventually taking over the business. His wife, Eileen, we called 'Mrs Lala' and she served in the shop and often gave me a free biscuit or cake, as my brother was a close friend of their son Norman. She often asked who my Primary teacher was, and was not averse to giving her opinion on her perceived merits or demerits. The other cheery, friendly face that greeted us there was Chrissie MacPherson. We simply called her 'Chrissie-in-the-bakers' to distinguish her from 'Chrissie-in-the-postoffice', Chrissie-in-the-butchers' and the many other Chrissies around the village. Mrs Eileen MacKenzie was later to become our 'Singing' teacher for a short time, in between permanent appointments at the school. She, and later, her son Douglas, were well known conductors of the Portree Gaelic Choir, leading them to many choral victories at National Mods. As an un-certificated teacher, Douglas was later to take Science classes at the High School. He soon saw the wisdom of reverting to the more lucrative and less stressful baking profession! (Our teenage joke was that he would now make more dough!)

MACKINNON
BAKER

SOMERLED SQUARE, PORTREE

Partners: A. K. Mackenzie — D. C. Mackenzie

Cakes and Shortbread a Speciality
— FANCY CAKES AND BUNS —
Try Our Pies, Sausage Rolls and Biscuits

ONLY THE BEST MATERIAL USED

For purchases other than the usual edibles we had to go 'down the pier'. Paraffin, nails, a tin-opener, a ball of string or similar hardware items were usually collected at J and R's. This was J. and R. MacLeod's chandlery shop on Douglas Row, at the bottom of Quay Brae. They also did grocery but we tended to be faithful to Lexy.

Willie Stewart's in Armadale House on Bank Street was also a port of call for hardware or knitting wool, flower and vegetable seeds, paint, wallpaper and a wide variety of necessities. This was also the place where we exchanged our 'winners' vouchers' obtained for success in the athletic events at the Highland Games or Agricultural Show. Amateur Status was very important in those days and we had to sign a disclaimer to acknowledge that we had never competed for money or indeed with others who were themselves not amateurs!

Butcher shops were in abundance, MacRaes' on Bayfield Lane, Archie Millar's on one side of Wentworth Street and Matheson's on the other. In addition to this, the Macdonald Brothers of Uiginish and Orbost Farms had a door to door service on a Saturday. Carnivores like us had a choice of the finest cuts. Vegetarians did not exist, or we certainly had not heard of such a strange phenomenon and a vegan was surely an ex-resident of Dunvegan! Our neighbour at number 8 Martin Crescent was Ronnie Matheson and he had a Fishmonger's van where we bought our cod or haddock. Ronnie soon went up-market and graduated to a grocery shop on Wentworth Street before moving both his home and business to Millionaires Row as we called Viewfield Road. Since then the Filling Station or 'Filly' has become one of Portree's institutions, the centre for all of Portree's news and craic.

MATHESON'S

11 WENTWORTH STREET - PORTREE
Tel. PORTREE 251 (2 lines)

Fill Up Here for the Outer Isles

Portree Filling Station

(Prop. E. Matheson)

Tel. Portree 251 (2 lines)

Agents for

LYONS ICES
BIRD'S EYE FROZEN FOODS

CIGARETTES
CONFECTIONERY   SOUVENIRS

Open 8 a.m. to 10 p.m.

SERVICE AND SATISFACTION AT ALL TIMES

Where can a gentleman buy a pair of trousers in Portree these days? In the fifties, gents were well catered for by Donald MacKinnon, 'Dan the Laundry'. At his shop one could get fully kitted out from head to toe. Fore-and-afts, cloth-caps, trilbies and felt Antony Eden hats were on display but I cannot remember ever seeing bowler hats or boaters. He also had off-the-peg suits and shoes, shirts and ties. In those days, as nearly all families attended church, every man had a 'Sunday suit', a complete contrast to the weekday working gear.

Donald Mackinnon

The best in ladies' & gent's clothes, footwear & school wear

WENTWORTH STREET
PORTREE

Telephone Portree 57

Next door to Dan's, Miss MacMillan's millinery shop provided a similar service for the ladies of the community. They bought fashionable hats for church, weddings and social occasions. Chrissie MacKinnon worked here for many years and eventually took over ownership of the shop when Miss MacMillan passed away.

How can I forget the delightful home-made ice-cream in the Caledonian Cafe. Robin Weir (senior), Flora and Norma MacLeod and Barbara MacGregor would prepare a 'slider' or a cone, perhaps a special one with a chocolate flake if we had extra pennies, for us to enjoy on our way back to school after a quick midday lunch at home. A quarter of Dairymaid Toffees was another Cafe favourite. For a short period the Calley also did takeaway fish and chips, but my favourite memory of this gourmet delight was from Jimmy Devlin's van in the Square, in the years before he built his takeaway cafe and shop at Bayfield.

Cathie Nicholson, who died a few years ago, was perhaps the last of the stalwart shopkeepers of Wentworth Street that we knew so well, as we grew up here in the 1950s and 60s. Hers' was the China Shop which stood beside Adam Hawkins' Chemist (from where Campbell, Stewart and MacLennan, Accountants, now operate).

C. M. NICHOLSON,
CHINA AND HARDWARE MERCHANT,
Phone: PORTREE 119   **WENTWORTH STREET, PORTREE,**
ISLE OF SKYE

Many excellent wedding presents were purchased from Cathie's shop, as she had a fine eye for quality crystal and china. The shop also stocked a wide selection of decorative paints and wallpapers. We could take home a couple of wallpaper books (2 to maintain a balanced walking position) to agonise over with the family, as Mum and Dad planned the re-decoration of one of our rooms. Such excitement! I was recently reminded that it was to Cathie's shop that families went to pay for their coal delivery. She was the agent for Beaton's Garage, the coal merchants, for whom she had once worked. It was also our monthly duty to collect the church magazines from Cathie's, but we were always pleased to call in to the shop for a chat at any time, as she was so fond of young people and was such a good conversationalist.

Mention of the Chemist's reminds me that the Co-op also had a Chemist's shop on Quay Brae, as well as a specific outlet for their bakery division. This subsequently became one of 3 locations for Alistair 'Bam' MacKenzie's Electrical shop. I'm tempted to say he did the circuit! Alistair and his brother had learned their trade in my Dad's business.

Later on, in the late fifties there were lots of changes in the shops. Calum Gillies, former manager of the Co-op, started a Grocery with his brother Iain, then later, a drapery, then a

M. GILLIES

Drapery — Footwear — Household Furnishings

Stockists of:
Gor-Ray Skirts — Lyle and Scott Knitwear
Windsor Woollies   Shamrock Knitwear
            and Ladybird

Agents for:
K Shoes, Van-Dal and Norvic Shoes

---

5 WENTWORTH STREET
PORTREE
Telephone Portree 5

A. HAWKINS
M.P.S.

Chemists and Druggists

Wentworth Street
PORTREE

Telephone Portree 100

MEDICINAL
PHOTOGRAPHIC
and
COSMETIC SUPPLIES

---

furniture store, each of them fulfilling a new need as the village expanded towards the heady status of town!

We remember the other shops and shopkeepers of our youth. David Forsyth's shop was on one corner of Wentworth Street selling souvenirs, sweets and books. It may seem bizarre, but we called it Billy's! This was because we loved the conversation and camaraderie of Billy MacKinnon who was usually the one who served us at the counter. Thankfully Billy is still with us these days, and provides a wealth of interesting reminiscences from his early youth as a Highland Games athlete and lifelong Portree resident. Indeed both sides of Billy's family were among those that made the village tick for generations. William Ross, postman and shoemaker, was his grandfather. No less a personage than the famous John Buchan, author of "The 39 Steps" said of him; *"The doings of Sergeant-Major Ross should not be forgotten."* William Ross was the 'father' of Portree's pre-WW1 Territorial Company who lied about his age to accompany the young men of the Skye Volunteers when they set out for Bedford Barracks, many of them never to return.

Dr Norman MacLean in his article entitled "The Hero", writes:-

"If many of these lads were far below the age-limit (one of them sixteen years of age, the youngest soldier in the great Army), the sergeant-major was far above the standard of the years. The story came to the village of how they were all asked their age when they volunteered for the front, and when the sergeant-major was questioned as to that, "Thirty-seven," he answered quickly, with a twinkle in his eye. In the evening the Adjutant turned to the Captain of the company, and congratulated him on the military ardour of his unit – "For the sergeant-major declares he is only thirty-seven, while he has a record of thirty-five years' service."

Across the street was the electrical shop run by Norman Beaton and his sister Mary Cameron. This had been my Dad's shop for a short time in the early fifties and Norman was another of his apprentices. Next to Forsyth's was Roger Gray the optician beside Archie Millar the butcher. Roger was a stalwart of the Mountain Rescue Team, CND (Campaign for Nuclear Disarmament) and a dedicated socialist at a time when there was a general suspicion of any person who showed left-wing tendencies. One observation that fascinated me was that Roger, a pacifist, limped heavily on one leg while his neighbour Archie, as a result of a war wound, limped on the other! To add to our name confusion there was another Roger who worked for Archie Millar and later married his daughter. Roger Jagger, the butcher, was also a stalwart, but in his case he was admired as one of our Fire Brigade volunteers.

Dad collected our daily paper, the Bulletin, from Hamish MacIntyre's, which was the only newsagents'. Hamish was another of the Wednesday afternoon golfers who enjoyed the meagre facilities at Portree's nine-hole course. We also remember the friendly ladies in the Cuchuillin Handloom shop. Donald Matheson (Dolan), bustled about on the opposite side of the street. He was always keen to ask me, or my brothers, of things happening at the school. Education was his first love though his time as a teacher must have proved difficult, as many of the pupils took advantage of his good nature and eccentric ways. My brother Duncan may have been one of the worst culprits. "Now watch the board while I go through it", was his customary expression, but his super-powers always failed to live up to this promise! Dolan gave up his teaching to rescue his father's ailing butcher's business. Not only did he rescue it, he died a millionaire, when such status was in short supply in the country. He branched out into breeding high quality animals to fulfil the requirements of the business and shrewdly acquired land when prices were low. He and his sister Chrissie lived frugally, probably not realising the value of their assets. All these people were superior members of the community who commanded great respect. I'm reminded that Dolan was persuaded to stand for the District Council along with 'Pop' Urquhart. They are both remembered by the street-names Matheson Place and Urquhart Place. Dolan was very keen that Skye should be linked with the Western Isles Council authority as we had been marginalised so long by Inverness-shire. Our experience since, with Highland Council, has taught us that this butcher was a sharper blade than his colleagues!

When in Portree visit

FRASER MACINTYRE

Newsagent, Stationer, Gaelic and English Literature
Fishing Tackle, Tobacconist

(Wholesale and Retail)

We invite you to visit our Toy Showroom

14 WENTWORTH STREET
TELEPHONE PORTREE 18

BEEF

FOR PRIME —
MUTTON

PORK

Shop at

M. MATHESON

BUTCHERS AND POULTERERS

Tel : Portree 51

VAN DELIVERY SERVICE

Roasting Chickens   Boiling Fowls
Quick Frozen Foods

Visit our Restaurant when at Portree

While on the subject of food and clothing, I recall that, in common with most of my male contemporaries, I wore only shorts while in Primary School. Longs were for big boys in Secondary! I can remember one pupil and one teacher who regularly came to school in the kilt.

In winter I often nagged my parents for boots – not just any boots but 'tackety' boots. How I envied the lads who could strike sparks from the pavement.

CHAPTER 8

Names, Nicknames, Patronymics and Acronyms

As Portree emerged reluctantly into an English speaking cosmopolitan world in the 1950s we began to witness surnames which were hitherto unknown in the area. Most of us were Macdonalds, MacLeods, MacKinnons, MacSweens and Nicolsons with a sprinkling of Mathesons, Beatons and Stewarts. As our forenames were also commonly restricted to Donalds, Johns, Calums, Duncans and Ruaraidhs, we were reliant on other means of identifying each other accurately. The incomers were easy and forenames for them were unnecessary encumbrances. 'Caird' and 'Gourdie' had a plumbers' business, 'Campkin' was the French teacher, 'Marr' was the 'Cruelty' (i.e. SSPCA man), 'Currie' did deliveries for MacBraynes' and 'Souter' was the Road Surveyor. We knew his Christian name was Ian but, as he was the only Souter around, we dispensed with it entirely. When his son, also Ian, grew up amongst us, with a touch of irony we called him 'Mac'. There were one or two folk who had unusual forenames so these were sufficient for instant identification. 'Claude' was the painter, 'Albert' one of the butchers and 'Sydney' worked at the garage.

Sad to say, if someone had an obvious physical disability, s/he was known by it. There was no malice intended in this, it was simply an obvious identifier. '*Alasdair crùbach*', '*Seumas càm*', '*Calum smotach*' were affected by leg, eye and voice defects respectively and so could easily be picked out from the crowd, as could 'Broken Wing' and 'Donnie-go-sideways'.

In common with most communities we linked people's names with their jobs and professions in order to better identify our target. 'Calum the Post' and 'Calum the Milk' both lived at Bayfield, so their place of residence could not be a distinguishing feature but their lawful calling was. 'Calum the Linesman' could be separated by job from the other Calum Gillies, 'Calum the Shop' and 'Kenny the Plumber' and 'Kenny the Butcher' were easily picked out in this way, but use of the Gaelic language and a study of *sloinneadh* (patronymics) was a better pin-pointer for 'Kenny the Butcher'. To our family at least, he was '*Coinneach Ruaraidh Mhòr*' ('Kenneth son of Big Rory'). His father had been renowned as one of the tallest and most handsome recruits to the British Army. He joined the Lovat Scouts and, like many of the Skye crofters, he took his horse with him to training camp. Called up at the start of World War 1 he saw action in Gallipoli and France. He was known as '*Ruaraidh Dìreach*' ('Straight Rory') or '*Ruaraidh Mòr*' ('Big Rory'). Kenny's brothers Neil, Calum and Johnnie were likewise known by their *sloinneadh*, so that '*Calum Ruaraidh Mhòr*' could easily be identified from the other five Calums we have mentioned above. Later, this Calum was employed by Sloanes' Catalogue Agency and, to us, he became 'Calum Sloane'.

However, we had another 'Big Rory' in our community, so he had to be named for his croft at Shullishader, '*Ruaraidh Mòr Shulishaidir*'. I remember the hay coils and corn stooks which filled the Shullishader fertile fields of late summer. *Ruaraidh Mòr Shulishaidir*, Roderick Nicholson seemed to us to be such a big strong man, except on the day he hurried into the ladies' staffroom in the school with blood pouring freely from his hand. While working on his field at *Seafield*, he had caught his finger in a machine for sowing grain. We later learned that he had lost most of one finger. As ghoulish young lads, we ever after sought to get a glimpse of his hand to see the damage that had been inflicted that day. The accident, however, did not hinder his diligent crofting in any way and he continued, like so many others of that generation, to work hard to make a living and keep his land in good heart.

Then there was the day of the Cross Country Championships. Farquhar MacLean, Teacher of PE, gave us our route and set us off. Up by the 'pigs' walk' at *Viewfield* to the white strainer-post in the forestry fence, then due north towards the golf course and back to school via the hostel road and the woods behind the school. All should have been straight forward, and progress, for most of the route, could be followed, as was his wont, by the sedentary teacher with binoculars from the sports' pitch. Duncan Geddes from the Isle of Soay had other ideas. He took a shortcut across one of Ruaraidh's ploughed fields and was spotted. Within the hour, the burly crofter was in the school office without the courtesy of a knock, demanding suitable punishment for the lad and the teacher responsible. Farquhar was called and explained that Alistair Douglas was in charge of cross-country running and Ruaraidh should take the matter up with him. Mr Douglas, the teacher of Technical Subjects, had nothing whatever to do with the incident, and was in fact safely at a meeting in Inverness on that particular day!

Inevitably, if we had Big Rories one would expect to have a '*Ruaraidh Beag*' ('Small Rory'). One of his daughters who worked in the Labour Exchange was '*Mairead Ruaraidh Bhig*' ('Margaret daughter of Small Rory'). Perversely we named her brother Norman, 'Malinky'.

Some of the many Donalds were given the diminutive '*Dòmhlan*' but they needed to be further differentiated and so Kenny the Butcher's boss was known to us as '*Dòmhlan Chalum Bùidsear*' as Calum (another one), his father, had established the butchery business.

On Windsor Crescent there were three adjoining houses whose residents attended our church. In the end house were a couple, '*Niall agus Anna Ceann a' Rathaid*' (Neil and Annie 'at the head of the road'). Next to them lived '*Mairi Mhòr Eilean Tighe*' (Big Mary from House Island, a tiny island off the coast of Raasay. She spun and dyed wool to make coarse, scratchy stockings. The mordant for the dyes obtained from the only domestic source of ammonia!). The third house was occupied by '*Ciorstaidh Mhòr Ùiginish*' (Big Chirsty from Uiginish, a township across the loch from Dunvegan). I remember calling at her house to collect blankets so that my Mum could do a spring clean for her. She gifted me a Bible when I left for university. These selected names illustrated something of our regard for place of abode, as well as origin, in our identification of individuals.

The features *Mòr* and *Beag*, were very useful but were sometimes given for more obscure reasons than for the overtly physical features of big and small. '*Donald Mòr*' was not always taller, broader or bulkier than '*Donald Beag*'. The descriptions may have been added when they were children. Donald, as a child, was only *beag* because his father, also Donald, was relatively *mòr*! On occasions there might be two boys in a family, each with the same Christian name. Not so strange really, because the eldest son was often given the name of his paternal grandfather. A subsequent son could be named after the maternal grandfather. From the restricted number of Christian names we have observed in this chapter, two Donalds or two Iains in a family were frequent. The elder then became '*Iain Mòr*' while the little brother was '*Iain Beag*'. I have seen families where the little boy '*Raghnall Beag*' grew to be a large fellow, outstripping his older more refined sibling '*Raghnall Mòr*'. This of course led to mind-blowing confusion in my young brain!

As previously mentioned, my great-uncle was '*Iain Mòr Aonghais Alastair*' (Big John son of Angus son of Alexander). My mum was known as '*Seasag Dhonnchaidh Phàdraig Nèill*' (Jessie daughter of Duncan son of Peter son of Neil). My own *sloinneadh* is '*Iain Sheòrais Shomhairle Sheòrais Iain Thormaid*' (Ian son of George son of Samuel son of George son of Ian son of Norman) six generations. Now that certainly makes for a unique identity!

Most of the references above have been to men's names. 1950s Portree was a male dominated society and many of the married ladies were simply regarded as '*Bean Chuideigin*' or 'So-and-so's wife' but maiden ladies, as well as gents, benefited, or otherwise, from some reference to a physical feature. Blair Douglas' song *Bidh Màiri Ruadh a' dannsa a-nochd* (Red-haired Mary will be dancing tonight) was not an uncommon saying nor an uncommon sight. We had one who lived next door to us! Indeed all her siblings were '*Ruadh*'. There was a Donald, a Willie and a Calum. '*Calum Ruadh*' was the well-known Gaelic Bard, a *bàrd baile* or village bard. He composed humorous and sometimes satirical songs.

Mention of maiden ladies reminds me of twin sisters who said of themselves in their rarely used English. "We're just a couple of splinters!" This malapropism fitted perfectly as a physical description. They were stick-thin!

Inevitably there was a '*Flòraidh Bheag*' and a '*Flòraidh Mhòr*', the former of which was a relative of ours and often gave me a thrupenny bit to buy sweeties, although she herself was very poor. Mum would feed her up with tea and scones when she came to *cèilidh*. I can remember a '*Dòmhnall Dubh*' and a '*Dòmhnall Bàn*' (Black Donald and Fair Donald) as well as one we called the '*Bodach Leith*' (grey haired old man). There was also the entirely bald man named '*Curly*'. Portree was a rich tapestry of individuals, each with their own features, faults and foibles.

Nicknames, both Gaelic and English were frequently used. A John Nicolson and his brother Ewen came from the Island of Rona to live in Portree. They both married and had families in the village. While Ewen was unsurprisingly called '*Eòghainn Rònach*' (Ewen from Rona), his brother got the nickname '*Cron*'. When we came to live at Martin Crescent we discovered that we had a very large garden to look after. My Dad divided it up into a number of plots for fruit bushes, strawberries, vegetables etc. As Dad was busy with his Electrician's work we found that we could do with a hand at potato planting time, grass cutting time etc. '*Cron's*' expertise with the spade and scythe was called for. His preferred language was Gaelic and he conversed freely with both my parents in 'the language of Eden'. He liked however, to make the occasional foray into English for the benefit of the children. I must confess that we ought to be ashamed of our amusement at some of his sayings. Neither was our own English perfect, and our Gaelic was much worse, but we did enjoy a good laugh. A much more public story is told of '*Cron*' prior to his Portree days. On the occasion of a court case in Portree Sheriff Court he had taken advantage of a space in the boat coming across from Raasay, with several islanders who had been called to appear. Out of interest, *Cron* attended the court and took his seat on the public benches. Much to his surprise he was called as a witness. His response was; "My lord, I didn't come here today. I came for messages!"

Cron's daughter Sarah went on to marry 'Bert the Slater' and the family all moved to Inverness. Our contact and friendship with them continued however and my brother Duncan took up lodgings in their home when he began his nursing career in the town (since elevated to city status). Several years later I taught *Cron's* grandchildren at Inverness High School.

If I mention that, among the Portree nicknames, one man was called 'Bash' and another 'Stab' you might be tempted to think that we lived in a community blighted by aggressive behaviour. Not so! For whatever long lost reason these names had been given, the titles had stuck and were used without offence or comment.

The bestowing of nicknames was brought to a fine art at the Elgin Hostel where all the new first year pupils had to undergo a naming ceremony following interview by a panel of senior boys. Some of the names were rude or undignified and would not have passed the European Convention on Human Rights but others were clever and perceptive and have remained with the individuals throughout life. A selection of these may be of interest to readers and may also bring back memories to some 'old' Portree folk.

Allan Campbell, who recently retired from an illustrious career in the Gaelic world was named 'Volt' as a result of his initials. Our former Portree pharmacist Donnie Alec. MacLeod, having arrived at school with a fashionable duffle coat was named 'Toggle'. Raasay lads and those from Uist and Harris traditionally received names of fish and birds! Hence we had 'Skate', *'Bradan'*, 'Cuddy', 'Fish', *'Crùbag'*, *'Giomach'*, *'Rionnach'* and 'Fry' as well as 'Skart', 'Plover', 'Peewit' and *'Druit'*. *'Adag'* was not an island fish, as he came from Carbost! The 'Seagulls', of course, were Mallaig residents. Was it ignorance among the committee that named an island boy 'Penguin' and did they think when bestowing the names 'Yorker' and 'Googly', that cricket was played in Raasay's green and pleasant land? For a number of years boys from Broadford were given names of alcoholic drinks. I believe this arose from the innocuous naming of Sandy Sutherland as 'Shandy', thus consigning his relatives to be for ever 'Toddy', 'Brandy' and 'Cossack' (as in vodka).

It was a smart idea to name David Hillditch 'Ben Drain' and this wit was repeated many years later when Jamie Vaughn-Sharpe became 'Von Blunt'.

Happy days!

CHAPTER 9

Secondary School

"The fine red sandstone building in 1948 which was demolished to make way for our current premises"

On the 11th November 1957, the Head Master, Iain M. Murray MA (Edinburgh) petitioned Sir Thomas Learney (Knight Commander of the Royal Victorian Order, Baron of Learney, Kinnairdy and Yeochrie, Doctor of Laws, Advocate, Lord Lyon King of Arms), that the name Portree High School, which he and the Education Committee of the County of Inverness had chosen, be accepted for Portree's Secondary School. The name met with the approval of the Lord Lyon as the school had "a persistent tradition with regard to the teaching of the Arts, Literature and Mathematics at an advanced level". It also possessed "modern and technical departments and has for many years fulfilled the function of both a day and boarding school with a roll of 500 pupils coming from the whole of Skye and the other Inverness-shire islands of the Inner and Outer Hebrides and from parts of the western seaboard of the Inverness-shire mainland".

The School Badge, designed by a pupil, David Forsyth was granted an entry "On the 86th page of the XLIst Volume of the Public Register of all Arms and Bearings in Scotland".

Its description is given as:

"*Azure (blue), within a double chaplet nowed of four Celtic knots Argent (silver), in a base surmounted by a dolphin hauriant (upright) Or (gold), a Lymphad (ship) under sail and flagged of the third, the sail charged with an eagle displaying gules (feathered wings), and in an escrol below the same, this motto EARBAM.*"

This was a proud day for the school and the motto 'Let me Trust' was appropriate. The badge was prominently displayed on the breast pocket of the newly instituted maroon blazers. A sky blue shirt or blouse, grey trousers or skirt and a maroon tie completed the uniform. It very soon became accepted by both primary and secondary pupils and was worn with a degree of pride well into the late 1980s and early 1990s when most schools had long rejected uniforms.

Why is it that now, in the 21st century, we so easily forget our history and best days and aspire no higher than the lowest common denominator?

The move from Primary to Secondary school was just as exciting in the early 60s as it is for pupils nowadays, but not as traumatic, because we were used to being on the same campus as the older ones and knew many of the foibles of those who were to teach us.

By all accounts, the staffrooms in the 'old school' were hives of fun. I say staffrooms in the plural, as strict segregation of gender was rigorously applied by mutual agreement. As pupils, we had no insight into the goings on in these places, as the teachers always emerged from them, in their flowing gowns after break, with due solemnity, but from the many tales I have heard since, they must have been supressing merriment as the craic was always invigorating. Our only contact with these institutions was the tangible cloud of tobacco smoke which emanated from them if we were sent to knock on the doors with a message. In there were many characters with powerful intellect, enthusiasm and drive, particularly in the ladies' staffroom. Mrs Nicolson, whom everyone referred to by her maiden name, Morag Lockhart, was stern of face but bubbled with mirth. Charlotte MacKay, in my time Lady Superintendent, a title reminiscent of borstal or prison, could also show the two faces that were at that time compulsory in the profession. The fact that the primary and secondary staff met in this way helped the unifying of the whole school into one unit, under one head, which was a huge strength in the community. Portree lost something when Primary and Secondary were separated and the recent announcement that the excellent joint-medium Gaelic-English, Portree Primary is to be replaced by two separate language schools is thoroughly divisive. Just as my Mum was punished for speaking Gaelic in the playground of Struan School, will Gaelic-speaking children now be similarly dealt with if they dare to speak English in the playground of the 'Gaelic' school? We cannot obliterate historical wrongs by blundering to the opposite extreme!

We were taught English, History, Latin and French in rooms around the "Old School" hall, but Maths and Science were in the separate "Science Block" which also housed the Headmaster's and Secretary's rooms. Ina Douglas was the school secretary throughout my time at the High School but she had succeeded Mora MacKinnon (nee MacSween) who had married my mother's brother, John Peter, known as "Nonnie". Ina was a delightful person whom we got to know only when we became trusted senior pupils. She played the piano at School Assemblies and at various functions. Her son Blair got his musical talent from both sides of his family as the Douglas clan were also accomplished Gaelic singers.

Art, PE, Music and Woodwork were, for us, in the fairly new "Tech Block". John Steele was Acting Head for a time, following the death of Iain Murray who had done so much to interest my brother Sorley in golden eagles and other wildlife. I remember the buzz about the place when it was announced that the new Headmaster was to be a native Skyeman, Farquhar MacIntosh. Like his predecessors he lived with his wife and family in the school-house, attached to the "Old School" and shared the tower with the old bell which I cannot ever remember hearing. (My memory is of the hand bell rung by senior pupils like Kenny MacPherson, Norman M. Gillies, and finally, myself, before electronics took over.)

The tower was later immortalised by my friend Robert MacDonald's superb 1970 drawing, days before it was so cruelly demolished. Why did we allow such a beautiful building to be destroyed?

Up through the school I had a series of unforgettable teachers: Latin with saintly Calum MacLeod and flirtatious Moira MacKay, Science with George Hodson, Robin Murray and Stanley Robertson, as well as a short spell with Douglas MacKenzie (the baker). His mum, Ailean was our "Singing" teacher until Mr Fisher and Mr Welford came. We seemed to have a different French teacher each year. Miss Smart, Richard Townsend and *Bean an Dòtair Mhòr* (Dr. Allan MacDonald's wife). I remember her often repeated, un-p c quip about the inhabitants of Trotternish; "*Rien ne bouge*" (nothing moves). "You all know the Budges of Kilmuir!" In Room 10, which was our French classroom, I sat at a desk on which was carved (in full) the name of our recently elected Inverness-shire MP, Russell Johnston, he had been a pupil at Portree High when his father was the Exciseman at the Carbost Distillery. Later, when I myself became a teacher, I was able to remonstrate with him on his bad example. He enjoyed the tale immensely but was reluctant to accept responsibility. He was a politician after all!

Ian Willoughby taught us Woodwork. Do you remember him telling us to put our blazers over our heads, as if in a submarine, hold one sleeve like a periscope; "close the hatches", "dive, dive, dive", as he poured water down the sleeve? "I told you to close the hatches!!"

My Chemistry teacher Stanley Robertson's professionalism must have had a positive influence on me so that I followed in his footsteps. He was later to be my boss, close colleague and friend.

For Art we had the gruff John 'Knocky' Macdonald ("if you misbehave I'll knock your block off") we did not dare to test him!; for Arithmetic the fierce Mrs MacInnes ('Sadie', "take a hundred lines") who later, out of school, proved to be the nicest, gentlest and kindest lady; and little did I realise that several of these would later be my colleagues when I returned in 1980 to teach at Portree. For different reasons I particularly remember the arrival of certain female staff members. The flamboyant and truly inspiring Margaret Penrose (later Methven), my good friend and mentor the lovely Janet MacLeod and a young man's fancy Janice Dickie.

Robin Murray and later Alistair Turner, Renee MacLeod and Forrest Moffat were a great influence on the outdoor side of my schooling and Field Trips, excursions to Torrin and Athletics at Inverness, Dingwall, Gordonstoun and Glasgow are remembered as wonderful experiences made possible by the unpaid dedication of these great examples of a caring profession. We had a succession of History teachers; the actor Robert Cameron enthralled us at end of term by reading "The Para Handy Tales". If Dougie was here he would tell you! Mr Laing introduced us to Rugby and D. J. Macdonald

'Hero' got us through Higher, although he appeared not to exert himself too much! In S6, post-higher, for the first time, we actually studied some **Scottish** History with Neil MacKinnon known alternately as "Rabbit" or "Mooch".

My chief regret was that I did not study Gaelic in Secondary. On my first visit to France after leaving school I found my five years of classroom learning of that language could not help me to buy a bottle of lemonade!

I particularly remember the hall of the old building, complete with wall-bars, which was decorated so tastefully, giving atmosphere on social and other occasions such as mock-elections. We also associate the hall with Farquhar MacLean, 'the Bopper', head of PE, who requires a special mention, as he was regarded on a different plane by us lads. Past his physical prime, he could still beat us all at badminton, controlling the centre of the court and foxing us with deft touches for such a large man, but relying on his ample posterior, to prove a very 'dirty tackler' at football. As an ex-navy man he was very keen and skilled in gymnastics and liked nothing better than dusting down the pommel horse, spring-board and buck to set up a circuit. Boxing was another of his favourites but that did not always meet with parents' wishes. We certainly benefitted from an all-round selection of activities, sports and games but Farquhar's wit was something special. On one occasion, having heard staffroom gossip that a particular girl in our class was a skilled mathematician he asked her, with exaggerated emphasis and use of the required number of fingers, to collect 3 BEANBAGS from the cupboard. Another lad, flushed with pride at being the first of us to gain his driving licence at the age of seventeen, was asked to collect a wheelbarrow and take it safely and with due caution to the sports field. Deflation of egos was achieved skilfully on both occasions! Farquhar's antics as a hostel master are legendary but he received his comeuppance on one occasion while in shared accommodation with John Steele the Gaelic master.

On a cold winter evening, staring at an empty fireplace, as their rather mean hostess had failed to provide them with fuel, Farquhar decided that he would rectify matters. The school was only a few yards away and he knew that one particular outside door was never locked at night. Both the male and female staffrooms had coal-fires in those days and a full scuttle of coal was provided each evening, for the following day, by the ever efficient janitors. To reach these rooms and 'borrow' some fuel required him to progress around his own domain, the old school hall in the pitch dark. He could check progress by feeling his way along the wall where each classroom door was inset. Imagine the shout and jumping out of his skin as he touched a living person. A courting couple had also known about the unlocked door!

Robin Murray, our Physics teacher was another special, if eccentric character. One snowy day when the school bus, which he shared with 'Sadie' and several pupils from the Kensaleyre area, failed to turn up, he skied in to work on his cross-country skis, taught his numerically reduced classes and then skied home. He was, undoubtedly, a pioneer of learning through practical experience, willing to change his lesson to follow a scientific suggestion, by a keen pupil, to its logical conclusion. On one occasion he began the period by asking; "*Do you think we could produce enough hydro-electricity from the Mill Burn to power the school in term time?*" The answer required an expedition to the burn. We calculated height, flow-rate, average water level, energy produced, efficiency, potential sites for a mini power-station and eventually concluded that it would indeed be possible to power, not only the school, but also both school hostels all year round from this little stream! Why did I not immediately set up a micro-hydro business on the strength of this! Robin opened for us a new window on a wider world, while at the same time fostering a growing appreciation of the unique wonder which we had on our own doorstep. He loved Skye and wished us to understand that we were highly privileged to be growing up in this environment. The Mill Dam and Mill Pond, haunts of dragonflies and lacewings, were a source of tadpoles, and an introduction by him to our love of wildlife and a career in science teaching.

Another of our outdoor educators was George Moody. Maths teachers are not usually known for their love of the outdoors but George was an accomplished canoeist. We not only had the opportunity to canoe the canoes but also to make new ones both with fibreglass and by the older method of canvas on wooden frames. Our first excursion, once we had learned the basics in Portree Bay, was from there to Loch Sligachan. Although it was a lovely day with little wind, there was a tremendous swell. The canoes were so low in the water that I could only very occasionally see my companions as we were never sufficiently synchronised to be on the wave crests at the same time. On entering the loch we were in flat-calm water and progress up to the river mouth, with the Black Cuillins ahead, was an unforgettable vista. That same year, my fifth of Secondary, saw the first expedition to the old Torrin School. Portree High had been given permission by Inverness County Council Education Committee to make use of the redundant primary school, south of Broadford, as an Outdoor Centre. Electricity, flush-toilets and a hot water supply were all that distinguished this trip from a camping excursion. We cooked on primus stoves and carved baker's bread with a sheath-knife. Our task was to measure for bunks and complete some concreting work as well as to enjoy ourselves in the canoes. First we went up Loch Slapin to the Strathmore River and then paddled and portaged to the freshwater loch. Next day's expedition was southward from Torrin by *Camus Malag* and around *Rubha Suisnish* to Loch Eishort. This was my first view of the townships of Boreraig and Suisinish from which the crofters had been cruelly cleared in the middle of the 19th century. Our history lessons, although they had expanded on the doings of Clive of India and Catherine the Great of

Russia's foreign and domestic policies, had told us nothing of this, but the sad sight awakened a lasting interest in my mind. Later research revealed the harrowing truth.

"In the middle of September 1853, Lord MacDonald's ground-officer with a body of constables, arrived, and at once proceeded to eject, in the most heartless manner, the whole population, numbering thirty-two families, and that at a period when the able-bodied male members of the families were away from home trying to earn something by which to pay their rents, and help to carry their families through the coming winter. In spite of the wailing of the helpless women and children, the cruel work was proceeded with as rapidly as possible, and without the slightest apparent compunction. The furniture was thrown out in what had now become the orthodox fashion. The aged and infirm, some of them so frail that they could not move, were pushed or carried out. The scene was heart-rending. The women and children went about tearing their hair, and rending the heavens with their cries ...."

'History of the Highland Clearances' Alexander MacKenzie

Why was **this history** hidden from us?
This particular canoeing trip had quite a profound influence on me and a desire to understand more about my own people and land-use in Skye. At this point I still knew nothing of the involvement of my own relatives in 'The Battle of the Braes'.

I think I was only ever late for school on one occasion. It was February 1963 and that morning I hung about with others of my contemporaries in wonder at the devastation caused, the previous evening, to the historic Royal Hotel (MacNab's Inn where Flora MacDonald parted with Bonnie Prince Charlie). It was severely damaged by fire, which broke out in an unoccupied wing of the building likely due to faulty wiring (Dad never did work at the Royal!). Quickly the local fire brigade assembled, and brigades from Kyle of Lochalsh and Inverness were dispatched as well as all local units. For some time it was thought that the whole block which included shops and houses would be lost, and people and goods were quickly evacuated by whatever means possible. Bystanders were recruited, including the young folk. It was noted that the youngsters all decided to help Willie Grant, in preference to other shop owners, move his sweetshop stock to a secure location! Thankfully the wind dropped and changed direction, and the fire was contained within the hotel. The Royal was rebuilt, not to the original distinctive design, but still remains a busy, central hotel in the town.

In all my time at Secondary we lived and learned in the "Old School", the Tech. Block and one or two huts, but during my S5 we moved into the "New School" with our new Head, Mr MacAskill 'Eef'.

This "New" building was eagerly awaited. We had been subjected to constant noise and distractions for more than a year, as the steel frame was erected and hundreds of windows appeared. Jimmy Peacock was the time-keeper and tea-maker and Mr Nelson from Sleat seemed to have an important role. Higher English in Room 4 saw Shakespeare's "MacBeth" and Chaucer's "Canterbury Tales" competing with drilling and the revving of dumper trucks. How did our teachers ever manage to keep our attention? O grade exams were taken in the Elgin Hostel, accompanied by the loud ticking of an annoying clock. And then it was ready! Happy days! Senior pupils, feeling so very important as we helped the staff to move in!

But, was the roof not upside down? The pitch downwards! Surely someone had made a serious blunder! Who were we to judge our elders and betters!! Everyone else seemed pleased with this new building, later to be described, very aptly, by my pal Donnie Munro as "like a Soviet fish-canning factory". Did anyone complain or mourn the passing of the majestic "Old building"? Were we blinded by so-called progress?

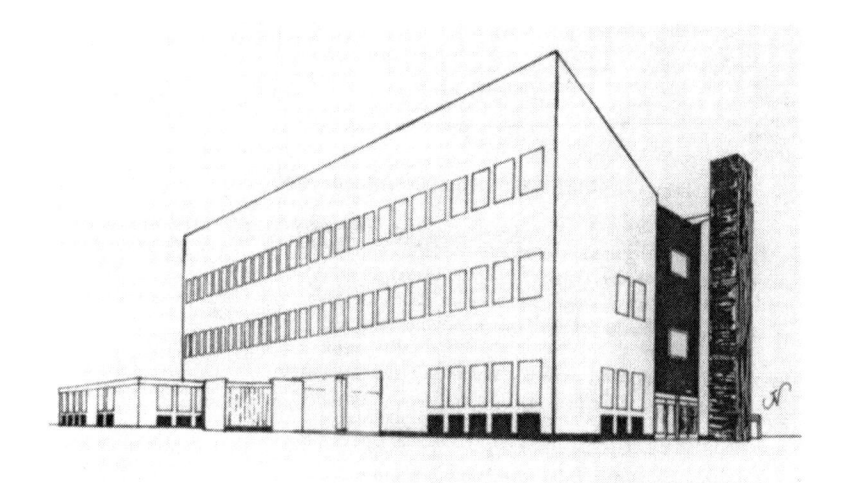

New Building—James Nicolson VI

We seniors only had a few months in the "New building" before moving away to be very little fish in a very big pond.

In retrospect, my schooldays seem to have been relatively free, fun but fleeting, although a very positive experience; and most of the bad times, which there must have been, have long since been forgotten.

Chapter 10
Crofting History in the Parish of Portree

It was in my final year at school that I began to take a personal interest in local history. I read Norman MacLean's book, 'The Former Days', which tells of his youth in the Upper Ollach Schoolhouse where his father, Kenneth MacLean, was the schoolmaster at the time of the 'crofting troubles'. Because of his closeness to some of the action, Norman had a good understanding of the unfolding events which ultimately led to the passing of the 1886 Crofters' Holding Act of Parliament which enshrined the rights and responsibilities which crofters throughout the Crofting Counties of Scotland enjoy to this day. His account, published in 1945, was however, written with a subtle slant towards the landlord's point of view, being dedicated to "The Honoured Memory of the Sons and Grandson of Lord MacDonald who died for King and Country." By contrasting his father's schoolmasterly attitude to violence with his own young lad's opinion, he was able to illustrate the ambivalence with which the Braes people regarded events. The patience of the crofters of Braes had been severely tried and, although loyal and law-abiding citizens of King and Country with an historic veneration for their Clan Chief, they had been forced to take a firm stand against abuse of power. Norman's version of events encouraged me to read more. Published in 1883 and written from the viewpoints of other "contemporary writers whose opinions are sure to command respect." The author of this 'History of the Highland Clearances', Alexander MacKenzie says in his introduction, "It is hoped that the portion of this work relating to the Social state of the Isle of Skye in 1882, illustrated by the Trial of the Braes Crofters, and other proceedings connected with the Island, will be found both instructive and interesting."

This was history on my doorstep, of which I had been taught nothing at school or even at home! I still wonder why. Were my folks ashamed that our relatives had needed to have recourse to violence entirely against their natural desire for peace and the biblical injunction to honour "the powers that be, ordained of God"?

The Braes

The townships of the Braes of Trotternish, mapped by John Blackadder in 1811, are Camustianavaig, Conordan, Achnahanaid, Ollach (Upper and Lower), Gedintailor, Balameanach and Peinchorran. The last three of these had traditional grazing rights on Ben Lee, on Lord MacDonald's estate. In 1877 these rights were leased, by the factor, for sheep pasture to a tenant, John MacKay, who offered more rent for the privilege than the Braes crofters could afford. Having witnessed the success of the Valtos crofters in forcing a rent reduction, the Braes men approached the estate factor with a similar request, since, without grazings, they no longer had the means to pay. Their polite request was met with refusal and worse. No longer would a crofter be permitted to keep a dog! Wood for house-building could no longer be cut on the MacDonald Estate without payment, and thatching material for their homes could only be gathered if the factor's permission was first granted. Matters had reached a very serious pitch. Some peacemakers in the community persuaded the crofters to club together and offer more money if their rights were restored. They did, but Lord MacDonald's factor said no! Many of the local men were employed in the fishing trade and regularly went to the south of Ireland in their open sailing boats. Here they encountered the Irish Land Leaguers.

Charles Stewart Parnell had introduced the idea of 'boycotting' and had thus given the English language a new word. The effectiveness of this tactic had led to Parliament passing the Irish Land Act, which gave security of tenure and legally determined rents. The men of Braes wished for the same. One of the Braes Crofters, half in jest, was quoted as saying: "We were having such good news from Ireland that we thought we would become rebels ourselves!" Some tenants decided to refuse to pay their rents to Lord MacDonald.

Inevitably the sheriff's officer was sent out to serve summonses on these offenders. They were to be summarily removed from their crofts. The local people gathered, took the papers from him, and ceremonially burnt them on the public road. This was viewed as the serious crime of "deforcement" and Sheriff William Ivory of Inverness felt that it had to be dealt with, quickly and effectively, before others in the Highlands began to act like Irish rebels. He summoned 50 policemen from Glasgow, the Chief Constable of Inverness having refused him, to ensure that the Braes crofters were brought to book. The morning after they arrived at Portree on the MacBrayne's steamer 'Clansman', they set off early for Braes with the Sheriff at their head. The weather, that morning of 19th April 1882, was miserable, with heavy rain and wind. On reaching Gedintailor, the crofters were rudely awakened. A warning message, however, was soon passed to the neighbouring townships, but not quickly enough to prevent the arrest of five men. Their purpose accomplished, the squad set off back towards Portree. At *Cuaig* the road narrows so that there is a sheer cliff to the right and a steep hill to the left. This was an ideal place for ambush. Although many of the male crofters were away at sea, their women folk rose to the challenge and set upon the 50 strong police force with sticks, stones and peats. Although the Braes folk were outnumbered, their forceful stand gave needed ammunition to a group of newspaper reporters, who had travelled to witness the 'rebellion'. The general public of Britain were given the truth of the grim treatment that their crofter brethren had been suffering at the hands of their absentee landlords and their agents. Sympathy was widespread. As a direct result of this 'Battle of the Braes', "*the last battle on British soil*", the Liberal Prime Minister, William Gladstone, set up a Royal Commission to look into crofters' grievances throughout the Highlands. Meanwhile, the five Braes men were convicted and fined at Inverness. Their fines were paid by the citizens of that town and they were fêted and carried back home as heroes.

By October of 1882, the Braes crofters had negotiated a rent reduction and had their rights to Ben Lee restored.

The poetess *Mairi Mhòr* did not fail to satirise Sheriff Ivory and 'the English' (presumably the anglicised clan chiefs), but is surprisingly reluctant to criticise the landlord's factor in this affair, as he was a grandson of the benevolent '*Dotair Bàn*' MacLeod. Sorley MacLean in commenting on this, points out that "*it was very plain that not one Clearance in Skye was made by anyone who had not a name as Gaelic as her own.*"

Perhaps it is no wonder that the education system, and Highland people generally, have found it hard to come to terms with the subject of 'The Clearances'. Too many 'natives' were implicated!

Napier Commission

In the spring of 1883 the Government announced its intention to set up a Royal Commission "to inquire into the condition of the crofters and cottars in the Highlands and Islands of Scotland". Not long afterwards, on the 8th of May, the Napier Commission had its first meeting to hear crofters' grievances. It was with great significance that the Commission first met in Braes at the Ollach Church and Schoolhouse. After a year of such meetings throughout the North of Scotland, a report was published which led to the Crofters' Holding Act of 1886. This was by no means the end of the crofters' troubles but peace would soon come. In 1897, the Government appointed

Congested Districts Board, began to alleviate some of the longstanding problems that the people were experiencing.

Since these times, the lot of crofters has seen many changes, most of them undoubtedly for the better. The definition of crofter as agreed by the Napier Commission was: *"a small tenant of land with or without a lease, who finds in the cultivation and produce of his holding a material portion of his occupation, earnings and sustenance, and who pays rent to the proprietor."*

A more cynical modern definition of a croft is:

'*A small area of land surrounded by exceedingly, and increasingly, complex legislation*'.

CHAPTER 11

Games and Sports

In the 50s and 60s we were very much outdoor kids. We did not have the indoor distractions that children have nowadays, nor did we desire to remain inside. Even in wet weather we endeavoured to find something to do in the fresh air, whether properly clad or not! School 'playtimes' were for 'chasing', 'skipping', 'peever', 'headers', shinty or football. Mention of 'headers' reminds me of the narrow pathway between two of the old 'horsa' huts of primary school. This place was ideal for two people to play 'headers', as the ball, whether tennis ball or football, could not go far astray. Usually we used a leather football with an internal bladder. Once blown up, the bladder mouth was sealed with a knot and the external covering re-instated by lacing up the leather with a boot-lace. On occasions, this operation was not as neatly done as it could have been, leaving twists and stray lace-ends. These, along with the heavy, rain-soaked leather, made 'headers' somewhat hazardous for eyes as well as heads. Much is made nowadays of boxers and footballers suffering from the effects of repeated blows to the head, we were told it might "knock some sense into you"!

From Primary School days we enjoyed endless 5-or-more-aside football games at what we called 'MacLaren's Field' on the Staffin Road, where the Millpark houses are now built. Of course the field did not belong to Andy MacLaren whose house overlooked it from the sidelines, nor did it belong to Kenny Morrison's family whose garage was our changing area.

It was another part of Dolan's croft and he was happy to allow us to play as long as no damage was caused. Our one and only away match involved the exciting bus journey all the way to Borve. That this was only about four miles away did not significantly diminish the status of the trip nor the enthusiasm with which we approached the match. We did however, lose count of the number of goals we scored against the opposition from MacDairmid School. I still remember the long wait for a bus back although we were able to stock up on sweets at Alec Borve's store.

I suppose our most skilled player was Willie MacKenzie or 'Willie Fixit', as we called him. Both he and my best friend John Angus Matheson became players of first choice for the Portree team in the Bagshaw League, others of us simply enjoyed the exercise and the craic.

As a youngster I was obsessed by speed and tended to do everything at a run. This is probably why I was not much of a success at inter-schools or inter-village football. I was unable to 'let the ball do the work' but tended to 'run with the ball' from tackle to tackle. Rugby was more my thing, as I was able to dodge and weave quickly, but I was in my 5th year of Secondary School before I discovered rugby's delights when a new teacher arrived and began coaching. One of our number, George Halliday, later played for Highland and was picked for the Scottish team on one occasion.

My brothers were both excellent shinty players and I thought myself quite good, but Mum curtailed my playing career as a result of my brother Duncan breaking a leg. The fact that this had actually happened while he was playing **football** seemed to have eluded Mum's thinking. If he could break a leg while playing football, much worse was likely to happen in the company of caman-wielding shinty players! As my early schooldays coincided with a period when Skye shinty was at a low ebb with regard to competitive matches, this ban did not create great difficulties for me. The arrival of Inspector Duncan MacIntyre in charge of policing in Skye, and the appointment of D.R. Macdonald as Gaelic teacher in the High School, saw a marked resurgence of interest in shinty both by adults and school children. Lads a little younger than me were to form the backbone of the most successful period in Skye Camanachd's history.

I loved athletics and had some success in sprints, long-jump and hurdles. Perhaps this interest began when I won the 'egg and spoon race' at the Primary 1 Sports Day. (Then and now I'm mystified by the name, as we used a potato not an egg!) Praise gives one a remarkable boost and I have found it to be a great motivator both for myself and my pupils in my teaching career. It was praise and encouragement from Farquhar MacLean, Annie Weir and Renee MacLeod our PE teachers which provided the stimulus for me to do well in athletics both at school and at university level and enabled me to go places and meet people that I would not otherwise have done. My first competitive excursion out of Skye was as a little lad on Primary 5 about to compete with Primary 7 pupils. We set out for Inverness on Alastair Lockhart's bus at 9:30am, as soon as everyone had gathered for school. We had teams of all ages up to senior level of Secondary and I was thoroughly spoiled by the older ones. The journey took all day due to ferry queues at Kyleakin, several stops to replenish water in the bus radiator, when it began belching steam, various toilet/sickness stops and a sandwich-lunch at Cluanie Hotel. It is astonishing that a trip which now takes only 2 hours 30 minutes by car should have taken so long then in Lockhart's bus. In those days the main road took us around the Moll peninsula, out by Erbusaig and Duirinish and over Carr Brae above Dornie. Quite a strain for the old Bedford bus. We eventually arrived at Inverness and were allowed an hour at the shops with strict instructions to be back at the bus by 5pm to be transported, girls to Hedgefield Hostel and boys to Drummond Park. Little did I think that twenty years later I would be one of the resident masters in the Drummond Park Hostel and a teaching colleague of Calum Cumming who was then the Hostel Warden. Next morning we

Portree Primary School Team 1960
John Lockhart, the author, Charles MacLeod,
Agnes Bruce, Grigor Cup, Sarah Macdonald.

were driven to the Bught Park to start our competitions. Imagine the mixture of excitement and nervous anticipation as we waited for the morning's heats. I ran in both the 100 and 200 yards races and was astonished to win both the heats and the afternoon finals and our mixed boys-girls team won the 4 X 100 yards relay. The points tally meant that we had won the Grigor cup while a Secondary team collected the Annie MacKinnon trophy. Not a little 'big-headed' after this event it was my older siblings who inevitably deflated my ego!

This success stimulated interest and I, along with several other pupils began to train for events, a thing which was fairly unknown at that time. North of Scotland records in hurdles and long-jump were to follow. As a direct result of serious training, our school athletics teams brought home a series of trophies from mainland competitions, culminating in the

Donald MacKenzie, Alastair Gillies, Hugh Macdonald, Donnie MacQueen. Donald MacSween, the author, Graham Honey.

defeat of Gordonstoun Academy senior team at the North of Scotland Schools Sports, much to their aristocratic chagrin and our plebeian delight. This prestigious event was closely followed by our rugby sevens' team destroying north champions, Invergordon Academy by 27 points to 9.

Athletics competitions took me to Aberdeen, Glasgow, Edinburgh, Durham, Belfast and Dublin with mixed success but great enjoyment.

In the early 1960s we had several snowy winters and sledging took off as the 'in' activity. Dolan's field was the place to be! I had got a 'Yankee Clipper' sledge for a birthday present and speed competitions began. The track was not exactly ideal as there was the hazard of the 'slaughter house' to be negotiated lest it should live up to its name! As I observe this field now, covered in rushes, gorse and tussocks of grass, it does not look at all like the smooth piste we enjoyed. For a dare we once started on our sledges from the top of Fraser Crescent (no sleeping policemen then) and travelled at a variety of speeds down Stormy Hill and Quay Brae to the pier. The very thought of a grandchild of mine attempting such a thing now makes me cringe. Roads were quieter in those days of course and the snowy conditions meant that most motorists had the good sense to stay indoors, but one lad claimed to have gone right under a lorry. Fortunately it was **parked** on Quay Brae at the time!

Carts or Bogies were the next craze. A cousin of my Mum's made my first one for me and for many seasons I strove to improve and perfect it. Mac Souter had the best bogie around as his had a steering wheel and brakes. My brakes were the heels of my shoes and an occasional knee! Cuts and grazes were common place and were often regarded as a badge of pride.

For a while we took to archery and thankfully we all survived. At the tower 'up-the-lump' there was a patch of vegetation we regarded as a source of ready-made arrows. As I look back I realise that we were not as careful as we ought to have been. This was also the case in the catapult season. A forked hazel branch of suitable dimensions was chosen in the woods behind the school, in what we called 'Sleepy Valley', and cut to size, a punctured rubber inner-tube from a tyre was scrounged from the boys at the garage and a powerful weapon was constructed. Did we cause damage around the area? I'm sure some lads set out to do so but most of us were simply careless. After a build-up of rows from parents another adventure would be substituted as a replacement. In autumn this would usually be 'conkers'! Nuts from the horse-chestnut tree were dried in the oven and threaded on a string. You then felt able to challenge a friend in order to conquer his 'conker'. Victory was gained by breaking your opponent's nut (not his head) and a series of such successes meant that your conker gained status until it was supreme or was ultimately defeated, to your great disappointment and a pledge to prepare an even better one. I remember that one chap had remarkable success by pickling his conker in vinegar overnight. There were not many horse-chestnut trees around Portree but we knew exactly where they were. There was one at the top corner of the school sports field, one or two 'up-the-lump' and one in Sammy-Hammy's garden. Samuel Hamilton was the Factor for the Department of Agriculture Estates and lived in the large Scorrybreak House. We were not deterred by his status when entering the garden to collect the best conkers. One of the lads who ran around with us at this time was none other than Donnie Munro who, as a result of his career success with the band Runrig, is now the **owner** of Sorrybreak House. Are today's young folk enterprising enough to gather conkers in his garden and, if so, is he as tolerant of the aspirations of youth as Sammy-Hammy was?

In summer we played a similar game with the seed-heads of certain grasses which we called 'soldiers'. Are today's kids missing out on these simple pursuits or do they just laugh at our country ways?

When Willie Stewart decided to improve the paving outside his shop at Armadale House, a very smooth sloping surface was the result. We all got roller skates. These were not the in-line-wheel boots which are now available but metal structures which were strapped over our shoes. Each had four wheels and **no** support for joints. Great fun but several sprained ankles was the result!

For a few weeks each summer the craze for tennis was rekindled by the commentaries from Wimbledon avidly listened to on the radio. In those days we had a tarmacadam tennis court and clubhouse beside the telephone exchange. I have a notion that we paid for a tennis session, but how much and to whom I cannot remember. I do remember the sundial at the entrance to the courts dedicated to a Dr R. C. Scott, former GP, which, in 1936 was erected, by the club, in his memory. Miss Toonie MacDonald of Viewfield had performed the unveiling ceremony. The question remains: Where is the sundial now? Did it also go the way of the Old

School sandstone blocks and the bust of William Gladstone from Quay Brae, removed in the name of progress and destroyed or purloined as a feature for some Council employee's garden?

Wintertime was for badminton. We played in the Drill Hall, the Black Memorial Hall, the Old School Hall or the Gym in the Tech. Block. There was no shortage of venues and we were encouraged and trusted to use them. We appreciated this and teenage vandalism was unknown as far as I can remember.

What of swimming? If an alien had visited some of our gym lessons in the late 1950s s/he/it would have been very puzzled at the antics of the class. Each of us, four to a bench, belly down and gesticulating with arms and legs. Annie Weir was teaching us to swim – on dry land! Butterfly, Front Crawl, etc. all got their allotted time. This was practise prior to our introduction to the canvas pool. Unlike the girls' changing room which had separate shower cubicles, the boys' was a communal affair. Into this wet-room Mrs Weir was able to set up a canvas construction, tied up all around so that it could be filled with water to about 3 feet in depth. By wooden steps, both outside and inside the pool, specially made for the purpose by the Technical Department, we could launch ourselves into the depths(?) for the real thing. What hilarity! From Annie Weir's point of view however it was a serious matter. "If you don't settle down I'll give you a pink skin!" She had taught in Stornoway prior to coming to Portree and was astonished that so many island children could not swim, especially lads destined to join the Merchant Navy. Lack of proper facilities made her take matters into her own hands. She badgered the Education Authorities, Councillors and Council Officials for many years before they were persuaded to build a swimming pool in Portree, paid for, largely, by the community itself. Indeed, I'm sure a fair proportion of the cost came from her own purse! She deserves to be remembered for her tenacity and genuine care in fighting for proper facilities. It was rather sad, two years ago, when the Portree Pool was ignominiously demolished at the Council's behest, with little or no reference to the struggle to obtain the facility in the first place. I found it rather poignant that the young man who sought to bring the matter to the public's attention was a great, great grandson of Angus Stewart, the first to give evidence to the 1883 Napier Commission on behalf of crofters in this parish. His words still echo down the centuries; "I cannot bear evidence to the distress of my people without bearing evidence to the oppression and high-handedness of the landlord and his factor." Substitute 'Councillor' and 'Council Official' into that sentence for a modern parallel! Community spirit, though on the wane, is not yet dead in the parish of Portree!

The local outdoor places to swim in my youth were named pools in Portree's three rivers. The deep pool on the Varagill, below the Marshall Bridge was popular, 'Spurgeon's Pool' on the Cracaig burn was closest to the village, but the 'Target' on the Leasgeary was well worth a visit. Swimming in the Bay was rather frowned upon, because of pollution I expect, but Camus Ban and the rocks at Battery Green were the salt water favourites. You will have perhaps noticed that this section on swimming seems less personal than the others as I was not too keen, having had a bad experience, in the company of some Glasgow boys, at the 'Target' as a youngster.

Golf was not my thing either but I enjoyed watching others, acting as 'spotter' and searching for lost balls to sell back to players. As young lads, we spent many of the warm sunny days of the summer holidays on, what was then, the small nine-hole golf course behind the Margaret Carnegie Hostel. My friend, John Angus Matheson, was greenkeeper as well as an outstanding young golfer. Those were joyous days listening to the singing of the skylarks, tutting of wheatears and the mewing of buzzards. The golf course was shared with a flock of quality blackface sheep, tended by the 'electric shepherd'. Calum 'the hydro' MacLeod was a full-time employee of Scottish Hydro Electric but also a skilful trainer of Border Collies. He often gave demonstrations with up to six dogs simultaneously under his control. His sheep kept the fairways in good nick but introduced unwanted hazards to the greens.

The overall impression that comes to me in remembering my active youth is of the freedom we were given and the trust that we had from adults. Nowadays there are restrictions placed on every activity, often for good reason, as the world has become a less child-friendly place and fear of dangers and strangers needs to be considered. How sad!

I've left cycling to the end of my list of leisure activities but it was one we particularly loved. No Shimano shifts or multiple gears in those days. You were considered privileged if your bike had even a three-speed gear. Most of our cycling was round and about the village or to and from school where there were bicycle-sheds. These premises were often shared with smokers seeking shelter from the rain! Along with those short and speedy trips there was the occasional foray into the countryside; the Peiness loop perhaps; Sligachan and back; over the hill road to and from Struan or the return trip to the Kilt Rock. If a day of glorious sunshine was chosen, views were magical and life seemed idyllic.

Neither then nor now had I or have I a love for sedentary and non-participatory sport. In the 60s, even our early television viewing involved considerable action on our parts! As previously mentioned, TV was late in coming to Portree. While much of north Skye benefitted from the Skriaig Communications' mast, we were hidden from it by the dominating summit of Cruachan. (Fingal's Seat is not the summit, according to a former Primary 7 teacher, Flora Macdonald known to us as *Polla Erchie*). A tall aerial on 'The Lump' allowed Alistair Bam to display a working TV in his shop window but this was not ideal for Grandstand on a Saturday afternoon! We needed to head for the country! John Angus's uncle Roddy had built a new Dorran house in a beautiful but exposed spot in Toravaig. Black and white reception for BBC and ITV (one channel each) was the best available. We were introduced to the novelties of the Grand National, the Oxford and Cambridge Boat Race and International Skiing, but only if we first girded our loins for a two mile cross-country run from Portree. After the results programme had finished we repeated our exercise with the return jog home for tea.

CHAPTER 12

Those Mean Streets

Until the 1750s, there were few houses around the bay, still known as St Columba's. It was Sir James MacDonald of Sleat, the 8th baronet, born in 1741, who laid out a very ambitious plan for the town of Portree. Sir James was a truly remarkable man, contemporary and friend of Adam Smith, and with a great aptitude for languages. His death, at the early age of 25, was a great blow to Clan Donald and indeed to the Isle of Skye. Sir James' outstanding abilities suggested parallels with the adopted son of Octavius Caesar, and so he has been called *"the Scottish Marcellus"*. His ideas for Portree did not come to fruition.

In 1889 the MacDonald Estate drew up a feuing plan for the village showing the existing streets and some of the named houses (Redcliff, Viewfield, Druimard, Druimgorm, The Chamberlain's House and Hawthorn Cottage). All vacant plots were consecutively numbered and tentative names were proposed for the streets planned. Some of these street names however, did not ever see the light of day, other than on the printed plan; names such as Back Lane, Sheep Fanks Road and Parliamentary Road have disappeared. It is noticeable from the plan that Alexander MacDonald, Lord MacDonald's Factor, Solicitor and chief factotum seems to have ownership of several of the houses and plots. Whether this was personal acquisition or in his capacity as factor is unknown!

The Courthouse, Prison, two banks (Caledonian Bank and the North of Scotland Bank), the Free Church (now the Church of Scotland) and the Portree Hotel formed Jail Square, later named for Somerled, progenitor of the Clan. This was the village centre from which the other streets were planned to radiate. After the First World War Thomas MacFarlane of Beaumont Crescent built the beautiful and prominent War Memorial in the centre of the Square. His son John was one of the many Portree casualties.

In my youth the main traffic flow was diagonally through the Square so that the cars kept the War Memorial on their right hand side. Ruaraidh Kelly from Braes had failed his driving test on several occasions. The main problem was his inability to reverse. He remonstrated with the driving examiner and explained that when he came into Portree he merely went around the War Memorial in the Square and drove home. He had no need to reverse!

Most of the early streets of Portree were named after the aristocratic spouses of the MacDonald chiefs, whose dowries, time and again, helped to extricate the clan from financial difficulties. Douglas Row was named for Margaret Douglas, daughter of the Earl of Morton, who married Sir Donald the 11th Chief and 3rd Baronet.

Sir Alexander, the 17th Chief and 1st Lord MacDonald, married Elizabeth Diana Bosville, daughter of Diana Wentworth of York, hence Wentworth Street, our main shopping thoroughfare and Bosville Terrace overlooking the bay. Lord MacDonald is buried in York Minster.

Similarly, in Beaumont Crescent, we see an example of a further link with the English gentry. To Thomas Telford's design, Captain Richard Beaumont, married to The Honourable Susan, daughter of Sir Godfrey MacDonald, had these substantial houses built and advertised them for sale in 1839 as "neatly furnished and well adapted for respectable families".

Connections with Clan MacLeod, Skye's other major clan, are noticeably absent in the history of Portree. The MacDonalds had it all sewn up!

All the other 'Old Portree' streets have functional names: Bank Street (formerly Church Street, because the 'Established' Church was built before the National Bank, but Mammon later took precedence), Mill Road (the road to the grain mill, running past the miller's croft), Park Road, Quay Street (formerly Shore Street), The Green, as well as the aptly named Stormy Hill. Bayfield Road had an even older name, *Rathad na Slignich'* (Road of the Shells).

One might be tempted to think that York Drive had a link with the Clan Donald names but its name commemorates the visit of the Duke and Duchess of York in September 1933. The other 'Royal' names Balmoral Road and Windsor Crescent were given to the pre-WWII Council Housing schemes. Other well-known Portree movers and shakers were remembered, post-war, in the naming of Fraser, Kitson and Martin Crescents. George MacKay Fraser or 'Wee Geordie Fraser', he of MacDonald and Fraser the solicitors and factors for the estate, gave his name to Fraser Crescent. James Clifford Kitson, a Yorkshireman, brother to Lord Airedale, spent most of his adult life in Portree, estranged from his wealthy family. He lived at Druimgorm, later to become the place of my great dental fear, and was known to Portree wags as

'The Honourable Clifford'. His name is remembered in Kitson Crescent. Many of Skye's Martin family distinguished themselves in the medical and legal professions. The best known was Dr. Martin Martin, youngest son of Donald Martin of Bealach, educated at the University of Leiden in the Netherlands and tutor to both the families of MacDonald of Duntulm and MacLeod of Dunvegan. He wrote "*A Description of the Western Isles of Scotland*" in 1716. It became the classic travel volume of that era. *Husabost House,* on the opposite side of Loch Dunvegan from the Castle, built close to the seashore, is still in the possession of the Martin family since it was purchased and extended by Dr. Nicol Martin in 1840. This doctor had lived and worked abroad for much of his life, principally in Demerara in the West Indies. He died aged 84 in 1885 and was the subject of one of *Mairi Mhòr's* laments. I'm not sure if Martin Crescent was named for Dr Nicol Martin or for his nephew Rev Donald John Martin. As *Mairi Mhòr* has been mentioned, note that she died at Beaumont Crescent, where the Rosedale Hotel is now situated.

The naming of Coolin Drive (and its spelling) also belongs to this time and, as it directly faces the mountains, was perhaps an obvious choice.

As I grew up I knew nearly everyone living in these streets and could link each person to their own individual address. The village was small and compact enough for a certain camaraderie and togetherness; at some times perhaps too much so, as we each knew everyone else's business. Such is village life.

The *Meall,* Lump or Fancy Hill, a natural amphitheatre (with a little help from dynamite), where the Skye Games are held, on the second Wednesday of August, each year, was laid out by *An Dotair Bàn* MacLeod, Chamberlain to Lord MacDonald. He also built the round Apothecary's Tower overlooking the harbour. This is the site of the last public execution in Skye. Angus Buchanan, one of the packman murderers, was hanged "*with the greatest decency and without the least disturbance*".

Meall House, once the local jail, a school and the oldest extant building in Portree, now houses the offices of *Feisan na Gaidheal*, dedicated to the promotion of the Gaelic language and Highland Culture. In my youngest days it was unused but was later taken over as the Tourist Office. By the time the visitors had climbed the stair they were willing to accept any sort of accommodation to rest their weary bones!

The old pier was an example of the design of the prolific Sir Thomas Telford who was instrumental in the layout of most of the quay area. Subsequent design work for 'Old Portree' was done by James Gillespie-Graham who was much favoured by Clan Donald, as he was the architect of Armadale Castle. The Marine Hotel was demolished in the early 50s to make way for the less salubrious fuel tanks.

As might be expected, the Scottish Episcopal Church in Portree is known as St. Columba's. In it was placed a stained glass memorial window in memory of Flora MacDonald. The subject of the artwork is *"Esther delivering her countrymen"*. The immortal words, *"If I perish, I perish"*, do indeed seem appropriate in the light of Flora's selfless efforts on behalf of the Bonnie Prince Charlie.

During my youth other streets were added at the West End; Viewfield Square was built around the 'new' school playing field, but Colonel Jock of Viewfield House was in favour of only the Gaelic name, *Cearnac Ghoirtean na Creige* being used. The two prominent Councillors of the time were remembered by Urquhart Place and Matheson Place.

Having named this chapter 'Those Mean Streets', I might have been better to have called it 'Those Clean Streets' as Tommy Jagger did a great job of keeping them that way. Tommy was a weil ken't figure who reminded me of Andy Cap from the Daily Record. He always seemed to have the stub of a cigarette in the corner of his mouth. A gentleman of the old school!

CHAPTER 13

Church Life

There is no doubt that Christianity had a considerable and positive influence on all of us young folk growing up in 1950s and 60s Skye. Most of us came from homes where God was acknowledged morning and evening in family worship. Church attendance, at least once, on the Lord's Day was complied with by the majority. A large number of children attended the variously named Sabbath or Sunday Schools. The school day at Primary School was begun and ended with the Lord's Prayer, and Religious Observance, as well as Religious Education were the norm. In some Primary classes teachers used the Shorter Catechism to make us aware of the various Biblical Doctrines. Bible stories and psalm and hymn singing had a significant part in our general education. Secondary School had regular Assemblies with a Christian theme and the statutory quota of Religious Education was Bible based. I can only remember school visits from the local Church of Scotland minister. I suppose he was the official school chaplain, as the Kirk was recognised as the Established Church in Scotland. (The Queen, or her representative, always attended their annual General Assembly in Edinburgh). There were two other Presbyterian Churches in the Village, the Free Church and the Free Presbyterian Church. As far as I was aware, the only other churches, where locals worshipped, were the Scottish Episcopal Church (St Columba's) and the Roman Catholic Church (St Mary's). Nowadays, although there is no shortage of 'religion' in Portree, and churches, with or without buildings, have multiplied to a stage that they outnumber the pubs, their influence on the community is considerably reduced.

In my young days the three Presbyterian Churches in Portree had their Communion Services on the second Sundays of March and August. This meant that the previous Thursdays were public holidays ('Fast Days') in the Village. Shops, and even the school, closed for these days and a period of rest was observed for fishing boats and on the croft. Through the 1960s this practice began to change, particularly in August. The tourist demand put paid to any mid-week shop closure; an extra school day off, so soon after the finish of the long school summer holidays was intolerable to the education authorities, and a desire by the churches to choose their own Communion dates, brought about a change to this pattern. All Sundays continued to be observed by the community as a day of rest for much longer however, but eventually the balance began gradually to swing towards secularism. Councillor Drew Millar tells a story of when his father started his butcher shop in the early 1950s. A lady from Bernisdale, calling in on a Monday morning, asked the new, incomer shopkeeper if it was his family's washing she had observed across at the garden of their Tote home the previous day. "No", replied Archie, "I've been well warned against hanging washing out on a Sunday." "Well, if that's the case I'll take a pound of mince please!" The implication of this conversation made it clear to the butcher that non-compliance with Biblical teaching and local practice would result in people's custom going to his rivals.

As most readers will not know about Communion Seasons in the Presbyterian churches of the Scottish Highlands, I will attempt to elucidate.

After the Scottish Reformation of the 16th century, Protestant churches were very careful in administering the Lord's Supper and in explaining the observance of the sacrament to their people. The Roman Catholic belief in transubstantiation, and other practices, formerly accepted in the pre-reformation Scottish Church were not to be tolerated. Services were held in a particular congregation from Thursday to Monday by way of preparation and thankfulness. Thursday, providing a time of peace and quiet from ordinary work, was a day for 'humiliation and confession of sins' and there would be two diets of worship reflecting this theme. The Friday also had two services to represent 'self-examination' of the fruits of 'grace in the heart', to encourage the true Christian, and to expose hypocrisy. One of these services was an ordinary sermon by one of the two assisting ministers but the other service gave opportunity to laymen to give 'marks of grace' and testimony of the change in attitude and life experienced by, and expected of, a Christian. This service was called *'an ceist'* or 'the question', as the men would answer to a particular Bible verse chosen by one of their number. Saturday was a 'preparation day' to prepare the heart and look away from 'self' and toward 'Christ' for the coming sacramental occasion.

Our family worshipped at the Free Presbyterian Church off Somerled Square.

This beautiful building was first opened on 16th September 1896 to seat 400 people. It cost £800 to build and at Communion times many folk gathered from all parts of the islands and mainland. Indeed, so many came for the Sabbath services in the 50s and early 60s that the Drill Hall was commandeered for the overflow. The morning service in the church was taken in Gaelic, while the other visiting minister preached in English at the second venue. After the sermon, many of the young children went home with a responsible adult, leaving sufficient room in the church gallery for both congregations to attend the more solemn part of the Lord's Supper. In the evening the languages were reversed so that the majority now attended the English service in the church. As the years went on, rather than relying on a let of the Drill Hall, the congregation decided to build a new Church Hall at York Drive. Most of the building and refurbishing was undertaken by the men of the congregation.

For many years Mum had several friends who were given beds in our house at Communion times. Sad to say I looked forward to these occasions more for the extra spread of good food than for communion with 'the faithful'. I had to make myself useful however, and was given certain duties, of which the polishing of shoes was my least favourite! Both men and women, in those days, wore black shoes or boots and Mum expected them to shine brightly when my task was completed.

I enjoyed the conversation of these ladies and gentlemen who seemed to have a wealth of inspiring stories from their life experience. Donald MacAskill from Carbost was my favourite. He had spent years of his life in the Merchant Navy and had a magnificent tattoo on his arm. I thought it wonderful, and imagined him as a pirate on the Spanish Main, but he was very keen to point out that it was a permanent reminder to him of the folly of his youth.

The Monday service of a Communion Season had a 'thanksgiving and renewal' theme and all the visitors then left for home.

These days the pattern of worship at Communion Seasons continues in the churches, much as it did in the 50s and 60s, but most Portree residents will have heard nothing of it, as attendance is now confined to a very small fraction of the population, although a warm welcome is extended to all.

Chapter 14

Adventures and Events

My first adventure occurred when I was in Primary 2. All the boys on our class were invited to a birthday party. I remember whose it was, a lad called Bruce Tulloch who lived with his parents and grandparents in Braedownie House close to the school. I seem to remember that this house might have been a church manse and that Bruce's grandfather may have been a minister, but I may have this wrong. I do remember that we enjoyed a selection of coloured jellies, exotic cakes and other fancy treats but the actual adventure began on our way home. Nowadays parents would be lining up at the party venue in their 'Chelsea Tractors' to pick up their offspring when proceedings had come to a conclusion. Not so in those days. As the party was in the immediate vicinity of the school it was not unreasonable for us six-year-olds to walk home as we normally did from classes. One of the lads, probably Hamish (Monty) Munro, decided that we should take an unusual off-road route. We capered down river from the road-bridge to cross by the rope-bridge. This consisted of two ropes across the stream, one for feet and one at adult head-height. Hazardous but great fun for little boys! Next we had to negotiate the 'jungle' in what is now the Bayfield car-park, but was then a swampy area covered with tall and dense reeds. As might be expected, our school shoes suffered somewhat and our posteriors felt the force of the physical reminders not to do likewise again!

When I was a little older, but still a Primary School pupil, we had a craze for 'gangs'. Nothing like the armed city gangs we read about in the newspapers but groups of neighbourhood rivals each aiming to make the best 'gangie', 'bothag' or 'hut'. As Tommy and Rory MacKenzie and John, Donnie and Angus Matheson were also Martin Crescent residents, and since we had by far the best site for a Guy Fawkes bonfire, 'Tommy's Gang' had high status in Portree and I was proud to be a member. As Tommy matured, got fed up, or became somewhat wiser, he deserted us for 'big boys'' adventures' and it became 'Knighty's Gang'. (It is interesting that, having only heard John Matheson's nickname spoken, I have never before considered its spelling. Much more fitting to think of him as a macho knight-at-arms than to contemplate the possibility that another spelling could have been intended!) We had several versions of 'huts' over 'Scorry' at this time as well as a very good one at the Shepherd's Bridge. On one occasion, Rory, John and I set off to walk beneath MacCoitir's Cave, around Beal via the 'Sailor's Grave' and 'Moses' Well'. Having gone round the 'Big Head', we discovered that the cliffs were impenetrable until we had travelled north a great distance. The climb up to the narrow pass (*Bealach Cumhang*) proved to be hard going and darkness was beginning to fall as we raced back down from Torvaig, by the back of the Coolin Hills Hotel, just in time to avoid search parties being sent out. No avoiding painful posteriors once again tho'!

COOLIN HILLS HOTEL

overlooking Portree Bay

PORTREE   **ISLE OF SKYE**

☐

All Types of Functions Catered For

OPEN TO NON-RESIDENTS

TELEPHONE PORTREE 3   **LICENSED**

A.A., R.A.C. — 3 STAR

Just in case you thought I had used a wrong spelling for the Cuillin Hills Hotel. This is how the owners spelt it in 1966!

Adventures continued however. A safari up the Cracaig burn, through the trees to set rabbit snares in East Park was one; sorties into the walled gardens at Coolin Hills and Portree House, to check that the fruit trees were being properly maintained, was another. Of course, as for all quality assurance inspections, sampling was a key part of the task!

Excursions with Duncan Geddes were educational. He knew so much about the seashore and its inhabitants and was a very skilled observer of wildlife. Some practices would be frowned upon in today's over-protective view of country pursuits. Duncan had a beautiful collection of birds' eggs in a cottonwool-lined box. The collection was built up with one blown egg of each species and he could sit for hours in order to pinpoint a nest for the next colourful addition to his wooden cigar-box. The Observers' Books of British Birds, Birds' Eggs and Wildlife were our amusements for rainy days.

Duncan had several solo adventures which hit the headlines. It was he who discovered the body of our former school janitor, who had had an early morning boat accident at the pier. On another occasion Duncan found the discarded proceeds of one of Portree's very rare break-ins. This consisted mostly of un-processed cheques which were valueless to the thief. I, and indeed my parents, were very glad that I was not present with him on these occasions, adventure or not!

In Secondary School our adventures were more organised affairs and were dependent on diligent teachers, willing to give up much of their own time. Robin Murray our Science teacher was an enthusiast for nature and, along with his wife Catriona, found and loved every nook and cranny of Skye. His School Field Club was perfect for my adventurous spirit and I loved every one of the trips.

Robin had been a pioneer instructor in outdoor education in the early 1950s before taking up his post at Portree High School in 1955. He was to remain in post, albeit elevated to Principal Teacher of Physics until his retirement in 1976. His wife, Catriona was an acknowledged expert on Skye's botany.

Her book, "The Botanist in Skye" was first published by the school. Between them they had a wealth of knowledge of the environment and a multitude of habitats on the island.

Our trips ranged from short excursions to their croft at Prabost to learn how to read Robin's many meteorological instruments – this was a subtle introduction, so that there were sufficient young folk able to record the daily weather statistics for the 'Met Office' if the Murray family were ever away from home. We also trekked up to a rain-gauge which he had us install on the slopes of the Storr in order to study the contrast between rainfall on the east and west of the Trotternish Ridge. Longer excursions took us to all of the wings of Skye. Robin was in charge of expeditions for The Duke of Edinburgh's Award Scheme and he set us tasks for all the levels. A three-day, two-night camping trip from north to south on the Trotternish Ridge in baking hot summer weather proved very difficult due to a lack of water on the ridge-top and fiendish midges in the glens. On another, low-level excursion, we had to endure torrential rain both by day and night; but we loved it! Another adventure associated with the Award Scheme was the series of First Aid lessons we had to do with the ladies of Portree's Red Cross. We had hilarious fun and I will always be grateful for learning important skills for life.

I recall one Field Club trip to *Sgurr nan Gillean* where Robin, as always, resplendent in kilt (at least as old as Colonel Jock's) in spite of the bitter cold, demonstrated how iron-ore in the rocks can cause interference of a compass needle. We then proceeded, in the mist, to go down the wrong corrie on our return to Sligachan! Lessons learned but in capable hands.

Other staff who greatly contributed to Field Club excursions were the kindly Alistair Turner, the dynamic Forrest Moffat and Janet MacLeod, whom I have already described as lovely, representing the Geography, Biology and Business Studies Departments. Alistair, an aeroplane fanatic, whose teaching classes could be transformed in an instant by a fighter plane passing over the school, particularly enjoyed our expedition to find the remains of the Flying Fortress which crashed into mist-covered *Beinn Edra* in the spring of 1945, with the loss of the eight American crew. Forrest always seemed to have boundless energy and showed us that not only the young folk could be fit and filled with enthusiasm. We learned much from his knowledge and character.

Work at Kiltaraglen was certainly both an adventure and a series of exciting events. Each year Alec MacIntosh sowed oats broadcast in a portion of his arable land. I have a vague memory of an instrument he called a 'fiddle' which he used for this purpose. The idea was to get an even spread of seed.

Harvest time involved scything the crop in late August or September. After a day or two we gathered the corn into bundles tied with a dozen stalks and stood them into groups of three or four to form a stook. When these were sufficiently wind-dried a stack was built up in the stackyard. A great deal of skill was required for this and Alec and his daughter Catriona were expert. The stack was arranged so that the winter rain would be kept from the precious seed-heads later to be threshed with a hand-held flail. Kiltaraglen always had one corn stack and two haystacks to feed the cattle in the cold months. It was unusual in those days to give regular feeding to the blackface sheep. These hardy beasts had to forage for themselves although some hay and turnips were provided if there was a prolonged snowfall. Scything of the hay crop was a task for earlier in the summer and it was a thirsty job. In the field there was a well with the coldest water I have ever drunk. Beside the well was always kept a large mug so that we could take a refreshing draught whenever needed.

The day of the Skye Agricultural Show was perhaps the crown of the year for Kiltaraglen farm. Preparations were made days in advance and Alec helped the local committee to set up the necessary pens on the King George V field. At home the cattle and sheep were groomed and made ready. Some years, if the number of animals to be shown was small, we would take them by tractor and trailer to the showground. How proud I felt, standing in the trailer with a cow and calf, two ewes and their lambs, as well as two cages with a couple of hens and a cockerel. Mary MacIntosh was proud of her hens. The family would also have entries in the vegetable classes, baking and jam competitions. Although I was a little chap in a confined space I seemed to have had no fear of the big animals. Was this bravado or ignorance? Other years, when I was older, we would walk the show animals, cattle and sheep together, to Portree. From Kiltaraglen the route was up through the Homefarm Fields, where the new Dental Surgery now stands, to the farm steading, then down *Rathad nam Banish* (Homefarm Road) to Springfield Road (at that time the track to Portree House Gardens), round the top of the park and then into the showground by the side of the Forester's House. This task was surprisingly stress-free due to a skilful shepherd, Wattie the superb sheepdog and a young lad willing to put his speed and agility to good use in blocking driveways and opening and closing gates at the right times. I'm proud now to see the new street-names in the former Homefarm fields; *Rathad nan*

Fhèoir, *Rathad nan Eorna* and of course, *Rathad nan Cìobairean* (Shepherds' Road! The Council sign 'Shepherd's Road' has the apostrophe in the wrong place). I know 'cos I was one of them!

Once all the stock had arrived it was time for a cup of tea before the sheep and cattle judging started. Most years there were rosettes to pin up on the Kiltaraglen pens as well as prizes to pick up for the hens, vegetables and baking. On occasions we waited for the 5 o'clock presentation of trophies as Alec would have another Best-in-Show cup to display on the sitting room mantelpiece. After their unaccustomed day out, the animals seemed eager to get back home and undoubtedly knew the way. Domestic animals are wiser than many people think!

Whether or not we had taken the animals back early or late, there was a full programme of show events for the afternoon that I was keen not to miss. I loved watching the horse events which, though amateurish compared to what we now see on television, were very exciting. The *'Duchan'* boys Andy and Willie were very skilled horsemen and I always gave them my support in the competitions. My favourite of these events was advertised in the programme as musical chairs for horses. It was their riders fortunately however, who had to find a chair to sit on! Each year the event was supported by various army teams giving displays of brawn, precision or both. Bands, both brass and pipe were to the fore. Then there were the sheepdog displays which gave visitors an insight into the work of the marvellous local border collies. Sheep and ducks were rounded up! Show-day was always a great day out for crofters, visitors and Portree residents alike.

Five of my Mum's family were still in Struan for most of my schooldays. Uncle John Peter ("Nonnie"), Mora and their children May and Duncan, had lived briefly at Balmoral Road in Portree but then had built Seaforth House at Coillore, overlooking beautiful Loch Beag, a branch of Loch Bracadale. The house name commemorated the regiment in which "Nonnie" had fought in WWII. Uncle Duncan ("Doodie") and

Peggy, with their children Ruari and Mairi, were at Struanmor. Bachelor uncles Willie and Ian were still in the old home, Craiglea with spinster aunt Daisy. We occasionally went over to visit and on three occasions I remained with them on my own for a few days. Willie had a physical handicap from birth which meant that he had a weakness on one side of his body which was compensated for by a very powerful right hand. His handshake could crush rocks! Aunt Daisy was very deaf and Ian suffered from an asthmatic condition. Although each had their own infirmities they worked their croft together and were able to take part in all of the communal crofting activities. As well as their share in the sheep stock club, they had a milking cow, or sometimes two. I had never been entrusted to milk the Kiltaraglen cows, much to my chagrin, but Uncle Ian was happy for me to have a go. I enjoyed my initial attempts, apart from being swatted by hairy tails and, with more practice, could have become reasonably proficient. The great attraction for me however was Uncle Ian's brown horse. I have a vague memory of travelling by horse and cart to the *Gàraidh Dhuibhe* where his cut and dried peats were ready for transporting back to Craiglea. Filling a cart with dry peat on a lovely summer day when one is young and fit cannot be described as work but rather is a joyful task. More happy days!

As mentioned previously, Mum always organised a week's summer break for us each year. Probably her insistence on a regular holiday slot was to ensure that Dad did in fact take a break from work as he seemed to be at everyone's beck and call. She also endeavoured to make our annual holiday an educational one. We went to various parts of the country, north, south, east and west but never crossed the border. Neither Mum nor Dad had ever been firth of Scotland! All of these trips were enjoyable in their own way but only one comes into the category of adventure. That was our one-and-only camping trip to Wester Ross and Sutherland. Mum, Dad, Christine, Sorley and I, complete with large off-white canvas tent loaded into the car, set off to the far north! Leaving from Portree, I recall that we had to cross on three separate ferries that day, to get to Kinlochbervie and Scourie. First there was the Kyleakin – Kyle crossing, then Strome Ferry to Lochcarron and finally the Kylesku crossing. All of these boats had a capacity for four or six cars only, and were loaded by a manually operated turntable mechanism. Queueing was viewed as a travel break and time for a picnic. I understand that nowadays there is only one turntable ferry operational in the UK – the Glenachulish, running on the Glenelg – Kylerhea route. The day's journey seemed endless and was probably made more difficult for the adults due to my constant enquiries about how much longer we had to go! At last we reached a place to pitch tent. Mum decide that she would sleep in the car and did so for the full holiday week. Our vehicle at that time was a Morris Minor Traveller with wooden trim and double opening doors at the rear. Actually very good for kipping in! This was indeed a great adventure for me but the fact that the family did not repeat it and sold the tent and camp kettle after this trip, speaks volumes!

Happy camper!

On a number of occasions our family trip coincided with my paternal grandfather's annual holiday and so he would come with us. He was in our company to Applecross, on one occasion and to both Harris and Uist on others. Usually however we avoided the whole month of July for family holidays because Grandpa always came up to Skye at the beginning of Greenock Fair and stayed until the end of Glasgow Fair. He was still a working man, of course, as he refused to retire until well into his 70s. Granny had died before I was born and this trip became grandpa's annual ritual. I always looked forward to it as I often accompanied him on his routine trips.

He had an early start on a Saturday morning to board a coach at Glasgow bus-station for the long daytrip to Skye. We would meet him in Somerled Square in the evening and drive him up to our house, hanging on his every word. A keen gardener, he always enthused on the quality of his now finished delicious strawberry crop and how his tomatoes would be fully ripe on his return south. How my mouth watered for the fruit I was obliged to miss out on! I marvelled at his doubly looped gold watch chain, which he wore on his waistcoat. The gold watch in his right hand pocket had a lid with a clever opening catch and Roman numerals and was counter-balanced by a dummy watch in the left hand pocket. He always carried his paper money in a large roll kept together with an elastic band. I mistakenly thought of him as very rich! Grandpa was altogether different from the other adults I knew. He made plans! On Monday we would visit Kiltaraglen and he and I would walk by the path at the top of Stormyhill. Each year this was the routine and Grandpa would be treated to a glass of *Stapag* (fresh cream whipped with oatmeal) and he would have a long blether with the MacIntoshs whom he had got to know on his visits when our family had lived in the farm cottage. Our route home was by the main road to complete the circuit. I had lots of boyish questions, in answer to which he added many historical and mythical tales. As his sister, Aunt Janet Robertson, lived at Waterloo, Broadford, he always spent

Our family with Grandpa on an annual visit

a few days with her and enjoyed fishing trips in Uncle Sandy's boat. Dad and I would chauffeur him to and from Broadford. As Uncle Sandy keep bees we always had the thrill of getting the gift of a honeycomb as well as gooseberries and blackcurrants from their garden.

Unlike my parents, Grandpa talked of politics. His version of current affairs always corresponded with that of the Daily Record, the only newspaper he would trust! (Our daily paper was The Bulletin). As befits an adopted Clydesider, Grandpa was a socialist. By contrast, Dad had rejected left-wing politics, as he had become fed up with the power of the Trades Unions when he worked in the shipyards. The kindness he received in the 'big houses' of Skye had moved his thinking to the right. I can't, however, remember any political antagonism between the generations, but Grandpa always bemoaned the fact that he, because of landlords, had had to leave his beloved Skye to make a living. In contrast to this, it was very clear that he loved Greenock and his work there. He was very fortunate in having most of his family around him after Granny's death. His summer visits were a joy to both him and I.

There were two other communal events in a Portree summer which proved attractive to young folk. In order to prolong the Tourist Season, those who decided those things, organised two sets of Highland Games at either end of the season. Skye Week was in May and the traditional Games Day in August. Often we did not attend the actual events on 'The Lump' but enjoyed the thrill of the bagpipes as the procession prepared to make its way to the Games Field. The August Games event had been established in 1877 by the 'great and the good' of the island to provide entertainment for aristocratic visitors on the days between the Skye Balls, and each event had become an integral part of the other. In 1879 the Skye Gathering Hall had been built to provide a venue for the formal balls, part of the 'circuit' of Highland Society Events. The formal events were not for the proletariat but did provide a couple of days of paid work for some local people.

My final adventures, before leaving home for university, included a short spell of involvement with the Skye Mountain Rescue Team. Richard Townsend and Ian Willoughby, two of our teachers, were closely connected with the organisation, at that time led by Pete Thomas of Portnalong. Our first 'shout' or call-out was on a late afternoon of beautiful sunshine. It was very exciting to travel for the first time in the back of a Police car. I'm pleased to say that this has been the only such occasion! We made our way, at speed, to Glenbrittle and set off towards Corrie Lagan. We each took a spell at carrying a MacInnes stretcher and a plethora of ropes and other paraphernalia. The regular team went over the ridge to find and stabilise the casualty who had fallen off a fairly easy climb clutching a large piece of rock which had broken off. As he was quite badly injured we had a long wait while painkillers were administered by injection and the man was brought back carefully to the *bealach* where we were awaiting our involvement. As night fell we were entranced by the beauty of the scene all around us. We saw the lights of Mallaig come on as the sun set over the Uists. That evening I appreciated the marvellous views I had of my island, perhaps more that I had before. The enjoyment was soon cut short and replaced by several hours of very difficult work in transporting the casualty by stretcher back to the awaiting ambulance at the roadside. Dawn was breaking when we arrived at the Sligachan Hotel for a much-needed bite of food. I have never forgotten that particular thrilling adventure. Other Mountain Rescue trips were much more mundane and mostly involved relatively low-level searches although there was one other 'adventure', to a walker who had broken a leg on the Storr.

After leaving school I did a summer job with one of the Council road squads. That proved to be very enjoyable indeed in the company of a group of very knowledgeable men, well-versed in Skye history, adventure and legend.

CHAPTER 15

Out and About in Portree

On any occasion that I chose to go 'down the village' during the 1950s and 1960s I was very likely to meet many of the same interesting people. The village was smaller then and I'm sure I knew everyone and, more worryingly, everyone knew me. I could not get away with any naughtiness without being reported to parents or teachers. This was a very useful check on the exuberance of youth for which I am now most grateful. It paid to be polite and helpful, as positive feedback could also be useful!

Often when walking down Stormy Hill from our homes 'in the Crescents', we would see older ladies carrying their shopping up homewards in all weathers. Helping to carry their bags earned 'brownie points'. There was one particular shopper however, who always declined help and we soon realised that the reason was that she feared that we might hear the clinking of the contents of her shopping! This particular lady had been given the nickname 'Half-bottle Flora'. As everyone seemed to use the name, I trust that her relatives will not be offended by me telling this story, indeed, knowing her origin, she may well have been a relative of our own and she could have been re-cycling jam-jars!

The eastern end of Wentworth Street and across Bank Street to Armadale House was the common meeting place for men at leisure. We simply called it 'The Corner' and I compare it in my mind, to the old photographs of the St Kilda Parliament, not because the matters for discussion necessarily related to plans for the day's work as in Hirta, indeed exactly the opposite, but the men at 'The Corner' appear, in my mind, to be similarly dressed, moustachioed or bearded and smoking pipes like the St Kilda folk. This was the gossip-place where news and current affairs were discussed at length, and a good waiting place from where the steamer could be observed passing the Black Rock on its daily return from Mallaig via Kyle of Lochalsh and Raasay. The 'Dotties' sold their herring here and veterans of the armed forces shared political concern at current news items, fearful that we young folk would have to experience the hard times that had come upon the previous generation. The survivors of the two World Wars rarely spoke to us about their experiences as they had seen and heard too much and did not wish to encourage our thirst for gory tales lest they would seem to glorify conflict. Memories of the loss of several young men from Portree were still raw when I grew up. While many of the island's soldiers, sailors and airmen had returned physically unscathed from World War II (many had been prisoners of war), Portree had suffered disproportionately in the First World War. Many of the adults we met around the village were indeed war heroes, although we did not recognise them as such and nor did they wish us to think so. A good example of a war hero and frequenter of 'The Corner', was the caretaker of the Skye Gathering Hall. 'Donald the Hall'. '*Dòmhnall a' Hall*' had been awarded the DSM for his distinguished service and courageous actions under enemy attack as boatswain on *SS Temple Arch*, a survivor of the PQ17 Arctic convoy to Russia. Only the DSC stood between the DSM and the VC in order of precedence for military heroism, but the DSC was only awarded to officers and warrant officers, so this man was more than just a Fire Brigade volunteer and janitor! Following his retirement from the Merchant Navy in 1948, Donald MacCaskill and his wife occupied an apartment attached to the hall and he kept the place in good order throughout the year. He also had the task of ringing the Church of Scotland bell at 11am of a Sunday morning.

Another 'regular' at 'The Corner' was Johnnie 'Com' (John MacKenzie). He had been a soldier, drove Alasdair Lockhart's charabanc and was recognised as an excellent slaughterman. John was the adopted son of Kate MacKenzie and her husband Ewen who was the Compulsory Officer of the Portree School Board (the 'duping-janny'; to dupe was to dodge school). The 'Com' nickname came from the involvement of a MacKenzie ancestor, a soldier in the Black Watch, at the battle of Coomassie in the Ashanti War of 1873. The family had lived at 3 Stormy Hill, but their house was severely damaged by fire. All throughout the 50s and 60s until his death in 1974 Johnnie continued to live under a 'lean-to shelter' in the ruin, without any mod-cons. He filled his large camp kettle from my Auntie Isa's tap and had historical tales to tell. We often wondered how he survived, particularly in winter. The throw-away remark that 'he was helped by Johnnie Walker' caused much confusion in my young mind as there was a man called John Walker who also lived on Stormy Hill. The 'helper' alluded to was not this person but the gentleman to be seen striding along on the Red Label!

We were always advised to stay away from associating with the men who frequented 'The Corner' and "had nothing better to do", as they were regarded as only one step better than the ones who always spent their time in the pubs. Indeed there were several 'citizens' of whom we were afraid because of their behaviour 'in drink'! Perhaps the less said about them the better!

If our course took us 'down the pier' of an evening, we were likely to see plenty action as the fishing boats came into port or left for a night's fishing. There might be *'Domhall Macfarlain'* and his sons from Raasay, *'Kenny Beag'* MacRae or the Staffin crews. The Corrigals, Tommy and Alfie, and John Angus MacPherson had new boats which appeared to be twins. At that time, the fishing from Portree, was going through a rare good patch and there was always lots of activity. Locals could experience much kindness as the men often gave us a fish to take home. Such gifts were always welcomed by our parents. 'Doing a good turn' was a feature of Portree residents for each other. As lads we were amazed at the skill and dexterity of Davie Sinclair who crewed one of these fishing boats. He had had a leg amputation which seemed not to hinder him in any way as he pirouetted across the slippery deck of the *'Eala Bhan'*. Brought up on a diet of Long John Silver, we credited him with all sorts of exploits. The fact that the author Allan Campbell MacLean, who lived in a nearby township, used a one-legged seaman character in his book 'The Master of Morgana' suggested to us that he was based on Davie, and we fancied we could also identify several of his other characters, **good and bad**, as people from our own community.

I have already mentioned the three 'Ancient Mariners' who hired out rowing boats. Our neighbour Captain MacKenzie was accompanied by Angus Matheson and Duncan MacPherson, known as *'An Duc'*. If we took one of these boats for a half-hour stint around the bay we would often observe Charlie MacLeod ('Charlie Bayfield') as he cleaned, painted and polished the 'Janet MacKenzie'. This boat was the property of the Northern Lighthouse Board and Charlie lavished much care and attention on her. His main duty was to transport the replacement lighthouse crews and their stores to the Rona Light. There were a number of homes provided on Bridge Road, Portree for the families of the keepers. The regular changeovers were made in all but the worst of weathers. The name 'Janet MacKenzie' is interesting in the history of Scottish lighthouses. Janet Nicolson, born in 1788, was married to Kenneth MacKenzie and they lived on the Island of Rona. In 1822 Kenneth and their two sons were drowned when their small boat struck rocks at the entrance to 'Big Harbour'. After this tragedy Janet ensured that a light was always kept lit in a window of her house as a guide to boats seeking shelter in the harbour. In 1851 Captain Henry Otter of HMS Comet commended the actions of the "philanthropic widow" to Alan Stevenson, Engineer to the Commissioners of the Board.

"Her cottage is on the beach and in such a position that a light in one of her windows when in sight clears all the rocks at the entrance of the harbour. For 10 years she has kept this light burning except on light summer nights, and in stormy weather when vessels are seen beating about, she puts up two lights.... Many fishing boats owe their safety from the storm to the poor widow's lights when beating up the Sound of Raasay in long winter nights and, unable to contend against the terrific squalls that blow from the Skye shore, they anxiously watch for a glimpse of the narrow belt of light." The Northern Board agreed to reward her "praiseworthy exertions" with a financial award of £20.

On 10th November 1857 a lighthouse to light the north entrance to the sound between Skye and the mainland was installed and commemorated its 150th anniversary in 2007. In 1970 I was privileged to sail to Rona with Charlie, on the 'Janet MacKenzie' for the last supply run before the lighthouse, like all other Scottish lighthouses, finally went automatic.

It is also worth mentioning that Janet MacKenzie was an ancestor of the several members of the MacRae families which had considerable business influence in Portree and Braes (and indeed still do!). Alexander MacRae, known as 'Guinea-the link' because he claimed that each gold link of his watch chain was worth a guinea, set up Portree's grain mill at Budhmor. Other family members were farmers, ferrymen and fishermen. Nowadays some have replaced the fishing net for the internet!

Charlie MacLeod was a brother of the better known Calum MacLeod, famous for Calum's road between Brochel and Arnish on Raasay. These men and their equally able sisters, brought up on a very remote island, were exceedingly well-read, corresponding by letter with relatives living in all corners of the world.

The arrivals and departures of 'the steamer' were daily occurrences but they awakened interest in a sleepy village. The morning departure of the 'Loch Nevis', later replaced by the

'Loch Arkaig' always produced a number of sight-seeing visitors and locals at the pier. This is delightfully recalled in J F Marshall's poem 'Out of Skye';

> "A lamp-lit quay that glitters in the rain,
> And by its side a steamboat waiting dawn,
> A flock of sheep with shepherds following on,
> Some tourists, heavy-eyed, then sleep again –
> Hoarse cries are heard; the silly sheep are fain
> To double on the gangway and be gone.
> No help: the dogs are on them, and anon
> They're penned on deck, still bleating, but in vain.
>
> The daylight strengthens, and the sirens sound;
> The last rope splashes, and the engines churn;
> The quayside fades. O misty isle, it seems
> As if no time to leave thee could be found
> More fitting than the hour in which men turn
> From sleeping, and, reluctant, lose their dreams."

I'm informed by Mike MacDairmid, boss at the Royal Mail Sorting Office that the old Post Office had a Steamer Clock on display, to tell the times when the Mail Steamer was expected to dock. That this important Portree Artefact is currently on show at the West Highland Museum in Fort William, ranks, in my book, with the British Museum's display of the purloined Elgin Marbles! Come on Councillors, get this transferred to our own Archive Centre!

Out and about in Portree we were sure to meet Donald Stewart known as 'Mandy'. He was a well-kent figure around the village, carrying shopping bags for pensioners or bringing the heavy packs of newspapers into MacIntyre's shop from the delivery van. Always keen to have the notices on the shop windows read to him, he kept himself up to date with everything taking place in Portree and showed up for a sneak preview at every event. My uncle, the Rev John Angus Macdonald, was

> In Loving Memory Of
> A SPECIAL MAN
> "MANDY"
> DONALD E. STEWART
> 1934 - 2002
> SADLY MISSED
> BY ALL THE FAMILY

heard to say that, when Mandy, as always, was spotted in the Square, meeting the late bus, "you knew that you were home". The houses at Stewart Place are named for him and his memorial stone in *Sronuirinish* Cemetery is particularly touching, showing the special place in which he was held by this community.

The name Bank Street remains today, but the predecessor of the Royal Bank of Scotland was the National and Commercial Bank in my young days. This is where I first opened a bank account with the bequest left me in granduncle John's will. The offices above the bank belonged to MacDonald and Fraser Solicitors. Among the many duties of Mr Philp, their head lawyer, was the factoring of what remained of the Estates of Clan Donald. My brother Duncan got his first job here on leaving school. No doubt he was just a gopher (go for this, go for that). He always spoke highly of the intellectual abilities of Donald Cameron, the other solicitor who worked with the firm. His abilities both in court work and particularly in Crofting Law were well recognised. However the usual local irony was turned on when he was nicknamed 'Dopey'.

In my mind I'm walking by the Royal Hotel and clearly I can see George MacGregor standing by the main door, immaculately dressed, poised to carry his guests' cases to or from waiting transport, including the barrowing of luggage to the steamer. I'm also reminded of George's prowess on the Golf Course with Hamish MacIntyre, Vicky Dan Ferguson and Willie Fraser.

I recently was given access to a series of letters from Hamish MacIntyre's brother Jock, living in Sarnia, Ontario, Canada, sent to his best friend Allan (Ellie) MacKinnon, Erisco, Bridge Road, Portree. These nostalgic pages make a wonderful read for anyone who loves Portree and its people, past and present. They have been kindly gifted to the Archive Centre at the Elgin Hostel along with a collection of receipts for work done on the house and garden by the bridge. Surely this remains the most beautiful garden in Portree, as it was from the middle 1950s. Allan was a well-liked postman and his wife Flora was always keen to have a chat with us as we passed by. My Dad did lots of work for them, beginning with the complete wiring of their new house in 1956. The total invoice was for £89 – 2s – 10d!!

A walk 'up the Lump' provided for a pleasant circuit with a good view over Portree Bay. When the tide is full the view toward the Cuillins in the south west is enchanting. Until the early 1960s most of the small crofts above Bayfield were well cultivated for vegetable production. Many of these crofts were resumed for the building of the hospital. Portree Hospital was opened in 1964 and has been a much-appreciated boon to north Skye. We very much fear that the latest plans of NHS Highland, to remove all the beds and reduce it to a facility for visiting clinics, will have serious consequences for the most populated area of the island.

A walk out to the School would take you past a couple of very busy places. Our Post Office and combined Sorting Office was the large building which now houses the Backpackers

Hostel. Red vans were always back and fore and the counter-staff were all well known to us. Portree boasted a postmaster who lived upstairs with his family, but 'Jonnaks', was usually front-of-house. He was John MacKenzie, another of Portree's recognised intellectuals. A tale is told of an American visitor, in an attempt to skip the queue, asking loudly if 'Jonnack's' perch at the counter was "the fast wicket". His reply, "No, this is the slow bowler's end", seems to sum up accurately both his wit and his leisurely attitude to the task in hand. John was very knowledgeable on environmental matters, an aficionado on Golden Eagles, an excellent shinty player and a leading light in the Skye Mountain Rescue Team. Another of the team's key members, Sandy Innes, was also an employee of The Post Office, but in the capacity of head linesman. Letters, parcels and telecommunications were all under Royal Mail control. The telephone exchange on Bridge Road was very important in connecting Portree with the rest of the world. A goodly number of local folk had employment there both by day and by night (only males were permitted to do nightshift). Winnie MacLeod was a stalwart among them, along with 'Big Alec' MacLean, Christine Nicolson, Catriona MacIntosh, Andy MacLaren and Gladis Cormack and lots more that I've forgotten. 'Big Alec' always came to his nightshift well dressed and carrying a briefcase. On taking his seat, he would open the case to remove his slippers, a newspaper and other reading material before settling down for the long-haul. An interesting fact I recently gleaned from a one-time employee was that smoking was not permitted in daytime but was after 10pm. Perhaps this was to protect the health of the lady workers on the dayshift, or more likely, as a means of keeping the men awake at night! To keep the workers 'on their toes', a test call from the mainland was put through to the Portree exchange at midnight and another at 3 am. If no replies were received, Skye was incommunicado until the first ferry sailed from Kyle to Kyleakin in the morning!

When we wished to make a telephone call from home, on lifting the receiver we would hear the operator ask, "Number

The telephone exchange

please?" There were no STD codes in those days, so you simply gave the town and telephone number required. "Fort William 2519" was a regular request of Mum's on a Saturday evening, as she called her sister Barbara for a blether. Of course, if the operator forgot(?) to unplug his/her headphone connector, all the Fort William news could be made more widely available in Skye! Not that that ever happened of course! My more likely use of the system was to make a call from one of the red telephone boxes commonly available throughout the island. "Transfer charge call to Portree 199 please". The operator would then connect to our home number and ask the person answering if he or she was happy to pay for the incoming call. If Mum or Dad was at home the answer would be yes of course but if one of my brothers answered, there was no guarantee that the call would be accepted! The more usual phone box call involved putting sufficient money in the coin slot to cover the transaction. When the operator had made the connection the caller was instructed to "Press button A", whereupon the coins cascaded into the coinbox and the call was connected. If there was no reply, the command was "Press button B" and your coins were returned with a clatter. All this interaction was with a real live human, someone you actually knew. Connection to India was NOT involved!

A tale is told of a lady telephonist from the Portree Exchange who married a local businessman. A telegram, or card, at their wedding reception advised,

> "Press button A, press button B,
> press all the little buttons you can see.
> But you will NEVER get your money back!"

Mention of the Portree postmen has caused me to consider them more seriously and of the key role they played in our community. Many were ex-servicemen and I'm sure they were part of the glue which unified the village, and indeed the north of the island. Not only did they bring letters and parcels from afar, but they distributed news both good and bad. If there was somebody ill in the house, the postman would call to chat and check, whether there was mail or not! I mention their names with an apology if I have forgotten some. John MacDiarmid and Roddy Matheson were usually in the Sorting Office. Roddy's brother Tommy, Calum Buchanan and Duncan Fletcher seemed to be the ones we saw most often in our street. Duncan's wife Margaret did much good work in the village and this has been remembered in the naming of Fletcher Place. Donald Graham and John MacKinnon both lived at Fraser Crescent and Robert Bruce moved into Captain MacKenzie's house as our next-door neighbour. Jackie Bruce, Robert's brother was sub-postmaster for a long time. He lived next to Calum Peacock, another postman, although one was in the last house of Kitson Crescent while the other was in number 1 Martin Crescent. George Stoddart, with his cap at a jaunty angle, was always around and doubled as a barber after Willie Fraser retired. The caring nature of these men and the regard in which they were held was highlighted to me recently when my attention was drawn to a letter published in a 'Scottish Field' magazine in 1979. The letter from Allan MacKinnon, then retired, was not meant for publication but had been sent to the editor for forwarding to a contributor, Alasdair Barke, who had written a poem on passing the abandoned home of the Macdonald family at Sluggans.

Alan wrote:

"After reading the article 'Lament for a Macdonald' in the January edition, I would like to say to you how much it meant to me. Firstly, let me say I knew the Macdonalds all my life, having retired as a postman six years ago. Although I did not enjoy going to the house on a wet stormy day, there was always a welcome waiting. The postman had to get a read of the letters, and the parcels at Christmas time were a joy to them; all the contents being shown with much enthusiasm. There were two brothers and a sister. The brother Angus was tragically killed by a motor car a number of years ago. He was eccentric but very upright, honest and always immaculately clean and tidy, living in another thatched building not shown on your sketch. A merchant seaman, he had a hard time during the war, having been torpedoed in the Atlantic – found unconscious on a raft days afterwards, and when he regained consciousness nobody could understand until an islander like himself came along, and understood the Gaelic tongue. Sister Morag died in hospital about two years ago; she was very crippled with arthritis. Alick, the other brother, stays in a home in Alness.

Two years after I retired I took a walk to the home which I knew so well. Like yourself I wondered why all the material things were left to decay, but understood no-one could interfere. The Macdonalds were a family who did not look for the material things of life; in fact they were beyond striving for them. How much happier and content they were compared to the agitators of today!

Thank you for the tribute you paid to these friends of mine, the poem and sketch were very touching."

This letter illustrates for me something of the social cohesion we enjoyed in our youth epitomised by the caring postmen.

The bus and taxi drivers were another body of interesting people with whom we came in contact. Captain Lachie MacRae took on a taxi after his retiral as skipper of the MacBrayne's steamer Loch Arkaig. He was my friend Iain's dad so we knew him well. Peter Macdonald retired from driving MacBrayne's buses and took a busman's holiday as a taxi driver. We knew him at church. Ewen Morrison and his wife Katie Ann were both in the driving business. Katie Ann did school runs for many years and Ewen was the driver for football and shinty teams on both long and short journeys which he made more pleasurable with his Gaelic songs. The Morrisons also attended our church as did another Ewen, '*Eòghainn Rònach*' the bus driver. One of the other taxi men was named for his oft repeated phrase "Dearie me" while another of the bus drivers, who lived on Mill Road, was known as Angus 'Sunshine'.

Donald Archie MacQueen from Braes was one of Portree's first taxi drivers. Often his car was left to steer itself home! I remember one of the second-hand cars he bought was bright yellow. Inevitably for the 60s it was christened 'The Yellow Submarine'. However on one occasion it almost lived up to its name. Parked on the sloping Bayfield Lane, with a faulty handbrake, while its owner sought refreshment in the Royal Hotel, it trundled downhill (perhaps helped by some local lads) until it finally came to rest beyond Park House in the Leasegary River, just by the stepping-stones. Luckily it was rescued before high tide. At the end of its days, this vehicle, abandoned to wind and weather, came to its last resting place straddling an old dyke at Achnahanaid and finally rusted away.

Mention of Bayfield and Park House has jogged my memory of the blacksmith's forge there. The smith was known as the Governor, and we, as little boys, were in awe of him. He is so well described in Longfellow's poem;

IAN GEORGE MACDONALD

*"Under a spreading chestnut-tree
  The village smithy stands;
The smith, a mighty man is he,
  With large a sinewy hands;
And the muscles of his brawny arms
  Are strong as iron bands.*

*His hair is crisp, and black, and long,
  His face is like the tan;
His brow is wet with honest sweat,
  He earns whate'er he can,
And looks the whole world in the face,
  For he owes not any man.*

*Thanks, thanks to thee, my worthy friend,
  For the lesson thou hast taught!
Thus at the flaming forge of life
  Our fortunes must be wrought;
Thus on its sounding anvil shaped
  Each burning deed and thought."*

Chapter 16

Those and Such as Those

Of course the 50s and 60s in Portree, as elsewhere in the rapidly departing British Empire, still had a few reminders of 'class'. Perhaps forelocks were no longer tugged by us commoners but we did realise that we had 'betters' who still deserved a measure of respect, although we did not always understand why. On Games Day, or at the May Skye Week we witnessed Lord and Lady MacDonald arrive for the festivities in their large black limousine. The registration number OST 1 did not stand for OSTentation, but for OSTaig, which was now their home, Armadale Castle having been abandoned for economic reasons. Times had indeed changed. When it was built, a single window in Armadale Castle cost more than a kelp labourer earned in a year on the Clan Donald Estates!

Major General Harry MacDonald of Redcliff and Sir Seton Gordon seemed aged and venerable as they led the parade to 'The Lump' on Games' Days. 'General Harry' was the landlord of the Braes Estate, to whom my granduncle John paid his annual £2 – 0s – 10d croft rent and we gave our annual tally of trout caught on Loch Fada. On the occasion of the marriages of his daughters, with the co-operation of the shareholding crofters, portions of the hill grazings were resumed and sold to the Forestry Commission. In return all the Braes crofters were invited to the celebrations. Relations between landlord and tenant had become amicable, unlike those of the 1880s.

Seton Gordon was a prolific author of wildlife and folklore books and a keen piper and authority on *Ceol Mor*. His observations and descriptions of birds and their habits are quite remarkable and they have had lasting effects on many readers who themselves have become writers on environmental topics. On one expedition to *Biod Ruadh* in Tallisker he writes; "On a grassy ledge of the precipice is the ancient eyrie of the erne. Its owners have gone; indeed there is not one pair of these birds nesting in Britain at the present day. The sea-eagle has shared the fate of the osprey and other of our rare birds." In fact the last sea-eagle had disappeared from Skye in 1907, before Seton came to live on the island and, although attempts were made to re-introduce them to the Inner Hebrides from Norway in both 1959 and 1968, these were unsuccessful. It was not until 1975 that the island of Rum had its first breeding pairs, but Seton Gordon had passed away in 1977 before these iconic birds had returned to Skye. I was privileged to interview him for 'Birds of Skye', an article the school produced for the publication "Skye 68".

Our favourite members of the aristocracy however, were Colonel Jock MacDonald of Viewfield House (*Taigh Ghoirtean na Creige*) and his wife, Evelyn. I have written some snippets about them in my previous books but make no excuse for retelling these tales here.

Jock was a much loved and witty character who, in my young days, was often seen around Portree wearing a threadbare kilt of the suitably named Ancient MacDonald tartan. Born in 1889, Jock attended Portree Primary School but went on, like Tony Blair, to Fettes College, Edinburgh, for his secondary education. Although, while there, he took up rugby and won a cap for Scotland, shinty was his great love. Jock became a tea planter and also served for a time in the Indian Army; he and his wife returned to Skye after World War II. His Gaelic, of which he was extremely proud, was as fluent as when he had left Skye as a youth. Immensely keen on piping, and no mean player himself, he was a stalwart of the Highland Games and encouraged local players at ceilidhs held at his home.

There are many tales told of the Colonel and his eccentric animals!

Ossie, the live owl, was often put into one of the large cases of stuffed birds which so impress visitors to *Viewfield*. While examining the specimens, one would become aware of a sudden movement or blink of an eye causing startled exclamations on the visitor's part and loud guffaws from Jock and Evelyn!

At one time, he had a large deerhound which followed him everywhere. My brother Duncan was Colour Sergeant in the local Army Cadet Force and had occasion to call at *Viewfield* to present a bill in connection with some event. The dog ate the invoice and the fivers which Jock had laid on the table!

Jock was often to be seen driving around *Portree* with tractor and trailer collecting food scraps from the local hotels for his pigs.

I'm indebted to my friend and former colleague Murdo Beaton for the following tale from his article on the Portree High School website.

"I will close with an account of an incident that took place during my 6th year at school and which will live in my memory for the rest of my life. I was called out of class one day along with two others – Murdo Gillies and Alasdair MacLeod – and told to report to the Headmaster, at that time Iain M Murray. Col Jock MacDonald of Viewfield was in the office with the headmaster and we were asked if we would go and assist the Colonel with a little task. Thus started one of the most hilarious escapades I have ever been involved in. We were taken to Viewfield House in Jock's car with his collie dogs licking the back of our necks and the windscreen wipers going at full speed even though it was a bright, sunny summer's day. When we arrived we were greeted by the sight of several very large pigs lying dead here and there – one was on the lawn in front of the house and another was in the rhododendron bushes at the side of the drive. We had to drag them to a large

hole in the back garden which Jock had already dug – they had apparently escaped for the umpteenth time that morning and Jock had, in exasperation, solved the problem by shooting them. The last one to be dragged unceremoniously to her last resting place was the one from the bushes at the side of the drive and every now and then when we stopped for a rest Jock would mutter sadly, "Seonaid bhochd, Seonaid bhochd!" When we had completed the task and were standing admiring our handiwork the Colonel looked across at us and said "A Pheutanaich, bho'n is tu's coltaiche ri minisdear, nach can thu facal!" 'Beaton, as you are the one most like a minister, say a few words!'"

As a schoolboy I also had experience of 'service' at Viewfield when a group of us were recruited to paint a corridor during a Friday Afternoon Activities, Community Service stint. I recall much hilarity, led by Evelyn MacDonald, as she showed us an original 'Thunderbox toilet' which was still in operation in the house.

As an old man, while attending a local funeral, Jock was heard to say to another octogenarian; "*Saoil an fhiach dhuinn a dhol dhachaidh a seo?*" "Is it really worth our while going home?"

Jock was for many years, until his death in 1980, chieftain of the Skye Highland Games and Skye Camanachd.

Given what you now know of our family, you will be surprised that we regarded my Mum's uncle and aunt as *daoine uasal* (gentility). Perhaps it was that James and Mildred Porteous had occupied St Columba's Rectory at one time and were thus somehow looked on as upper class, or perhaps it was because James was highly thought of in the village. He was the auctioneer and valuator as well as the ambulance driver and seemed to have 'a presence' about him. In my young days they lived on Stormyhill, in a Council house like the rest of us! They were the proud parents of RAF hero Flt. Lieut. William

Ford Watson Porteous, DFM, DSO and bar, possibly the most highly decorated Skyeman of the 20th century. Bill was killed on his 60th sortie, flying in a Lancaster bomber over the marshalling yards at Le Mans, France in 1944. A poignant obituary in the Oban Times, spoke of his being "*casual, quietly humorous and at ease with young or old, but bringing to every task, mental or physical, his contribution of quick appreciation and complete reliability*". It went on to describe a visit he had paid to his old school at Portree while home on leave shortly before his death; "*But one memory remains with many of us, a talk to the senior pupils of his old school, unwillingly consented to, but, of its kind, perfect. It was the product of a brilliant mind, completely unassertive, but delivered with a vigour and a sense of colour which set it beside the finest Service broadcasts of the war.*" For many years his photo rested prominently in the Headmaster's office in Portree High School. I, for one, was proud to see it, when our relationship was explained to me.

As well as aristocracy, Portree was blessed with a number of professionals and intellectuals with whom we had the occasional pleasurable meeting.

How Dr John Morrison managed to cope with the Portree General Practice as a solo doctor is very difficult for us now to understand. He seemed to be on call day and night and certainly gave the impression of being pleased to do home visits. Things are very much changed now, and understandably so, but are we less healthy, or do we just expect more from the NHS? As in the education profession, paperwork has doubtless expanded to take the place of primary care. Anyone who remembers him certainly does so with affection for his manner and professionalism. We also had a great deal of time for Dr Mary MacLeod who, along with a series of 'nit nurses', as we called them, dealt with all our jabs and inoculations during our school years. Portree Hospital was much appreciated in the north of the island although minor operations were the province of Dr Sinclair, and later Mr Ball at the MacKinnon

Memorial Hospital at Broadford. In the 60s and 70s there were very few middle-aged Skye residents with a gall bladder! Mr Ball's skill in removal of an organ likely to be a later source of trouble was legendary!

Our local NHS Dentist was a Skye native, Donald MacLean, known as 'Toby'. His practice was based at his home 'Druimgorm' on Bridge Road; although we always approached it, in fear and trepidation, by the back gate on Park Lane. His waiting room always felt cold, clinical, smelt of carbolic and unfortunately had no sound-proofing! Looking back on the many occasions when I suffered his administrations, I marvel that he had the audacity to support the CND campaign to 'Ban the Bomb' while harbouring so many 'weapons of mass destruction' in his dentistry arsenal!

Donald was a good friend of another intellectual, Derek Cooper, who spent long holidays in Portree and later bought Seafield House immediately across the Leasgeary River from Druimgorm. Derek, with his London accent, had been evacuated to his grandmother's house on Park Road during WWII and attended Portree School. He had an intense love for the islands of the north-west which is evident in his books 'Hebridean Connection', 'The Road to Mingulay' and, of course, 'Skye'. We felt proud that he was 'one of us' when we heard and read his contributions related to food and drink in the press, programmes on the radio and later on television. In the local hostelries many political and historical discussions took place between those two and with other equally able colleagues such as Martin MacDonald the Gaelic Broadcaster and Angus '*Aonghas Dubh*' Nicolson the poet.

Another of our professionals was the affable Angus Robertson, the physiotherapist. When we were young, the old Fever Hospital was his consulting area. My brother attended for some weeks following a football injury and received excellent treatment from that courteous gentleman.

In the early years of the 20th century, this isolation unit at the Ross Memorial Hospital proved very useful from time to time. The school log for October 1904 tells us that there was, "A whooping cough scare in the village — not many cases, but families are afraid."

In February 1910, there was an outbreak of diphtheria and a family of five was taken in for isolation. In fact, in a severe case of scarlet fever in 1914 the school was closed from September to December and the Christmas Holiday was cancelled to make up for the loss of schooling time! No long school closures in my time as a pupil, or indeed as a teacher! Schools always seem to be on holiday now that I'm retired!!

This hospital was built in 1891 in memory of Dr David Ross M.D., who single-handedly nursed his typhoid patients through 1887. He himself succumbed to the disease and died at Beaumont House on 24th December of that year. This man was certainly a hero of his profession!

For most of my youth our pharmacist was Adam Hawkins. He ran a very efficient and professional business with local staff, as did his successor on Wentworth Street. We were very remiss in our lack of appreciation however, and only now do we look back with regret because of the present day contrast. A long-standing staff member in the Chemist's was Ishbel, the wife of one of our two long-term legal professionals. Both had the surname MacMillan. Ishbel's husband was Duncan MacMillan the Sheriff Clerk and his colleague the Procurator Fiscal was Donald MacMillan. Duncan served the Portree Community faithfully for 40 years. Donald was the guiding light for many community groups and events throughout his time here. His involvement in local football was probably his appeal to us young folk, but he also helped to run local Mods and both the May and August Skye Games. His professional reputation went before him, as he had previously been PF at Lochmaddy during the War years. He it was who had the onerous task of dealing with the legal issues arising from the running aground of the SS Politician on the Island of Eriskay. No doubt it was from this experience that he learned the tact for which he became so highly regarded. He was masterly in dealing with local people who found themselves, sometimes inadvertently and sometimes not, in breach of the poaching laws. His name was often mentioned, years later, when many Skye folk were arraigned to court for breach of payment at the Skye Toll Bridge. We often thought that Donald MacMillan would have defused the situation without compromise to law or justice. Donald's advice was sought by the BBC when researching for the 1970s series 'Sutherland's Law' which starred Ian Cuthbertson. Some say that the programmes were based directly on Donald's professional experiences.

Another group of professionals were the Army Sergeants who lived with their families in the community and served for differing lengths of time at the Drill Hall. Each had his own approach to the job of commanding the local Army Cadet Force and enhancing the reputation of the three Services in Skye. How we admired their sons and daughters who had lived in different countries and could boast of all that they had seen and done. They made us envious and brought on a wish to travel and experience different cultures and climates. Much of their tales, of course, were pure bravado and in a quiet moment they would express the downside of a peripatetic life.

Perhaps we home birds were the best off!

Afterword

I began Chapter 1 with the two Gaelic questions asked of me by the railway guard, *"Cò as a tha thu"* ("Where do you come from?") *"Agus cò leis thu?"* ("And to whom do you belong?"). These are questions that adults all over the world ask themselves and sadly, many find no adequate answer due to man's inhumanity to man.

40,000 words later, I trust that I have answered both questions.

I'm a Portree Kid.

I belong here!

"And now, Lord, leave me not, when I
old and gray-headed grow."
Psalm 71 v 18

My other books now available:
"Like a Bird on the Wing" ISBN 978-1-906210-67-0
"On Wings of Skye" ISBN 978-1-907211-01-0
"Over the Sea from Skye" ISBN 978-1-78148-516-3

Lightning Source UK Ltd.
Milton Keynes UK
UKOW02f2016240815

257436UK00002B/37/P